HOW TO
STAY OUT
OF COURT

HOW TO
STAY OUT
OF COURT

by

Robert Coulson
Executive Vice-President of
the American Arbitration Association

Introduction by the **Hon. Arthur J. Goldberg**
Former Justice, United States Supreme Court
and Former United States Ambassador
to the United Nations

Crown Publishers, Inc., New York

INTRODUCTION

An avowed aim of this book is to encourage voluntary arbitration of disputes and thereby to spare our court system from unnecessary litigation. This objective has my complete support. All of my prior experience with the resolution of legal controversies, both as an advocate and as a member of the judiciary, has convinced me that peaceful, prompt, and just disposition through settlement or other voluntary methods should be favored by the parties involved, and also by the courts and by legislative bodies.

There was, in times now happily past, a judicial prejudice against arbitration, exemplified by the old common-law rule against the specific enforceability of agreements to arbitrate. The most quoted condemnation was that of Lord Campbell in *Scott* v. *Avery,* who ascribed the traditional rule to the fact that the pay of judges depended mainly, or almost entirely, upon fees and that the judges were opposed, for that reason, to anything that would deprive them of jurisdiction, and hence of compensation. As Judge Hough said in 1915, "A more unworthy genesis cannot be imagined."

On the other hand, supporters of the common-law rule have argued that this was not in fact the genesis of the rule and that the objection was not to the use of "these peaceable and domestic tribunals," but was simply a reluctance by the courts to hold parties to agreements which would have the effect of adjudicating their rights without protections provided in a court of law.

5

Whatever the original reason, modern courts recognize, as they should, that arbitration has the advantage, in the words of Mr. Justice Frankfurter, "of providing a speedier, more economic, and more effective enforcement of rights than can be had by the tortuous course of litigation."

I want to join Mr. Coulson in cautioning that parties should seek competent legal assistance in appropriate cases. The laws are complex. Increasingly, individuals and business-men need the experience and preventive advice of their lawyers. But the cost of prolonged litigation is becoming too great for many individuals to bear. It is this high cost which in part prompted Judge Learned Hand's observation: "After now some dozen years of experience, I must say that as a litigant I should dread a lawsuit beyond almost anything else short of sickness and death." And thus, the option of reconciling disputes pri-vately has become increasingly attractive. Clients will often find their own attorney urging that out-of-court techniques be considered. In such cases, the examples described in this book will have particular relevance.

I have long been associated with the work of the American Arbitration Association. As a former director of that useful organization, I welcome this contribution by its executive vice president to the fuller understanding of techniques for the peaceful resolution of controversy through the process of volun-tary arbitration.

ARTHUR J. GOLDBERG
Former Justice, the United States Supreme Court
Former United States Ambassador to the United Nations

CONTENTS

PREFACE

Our courts are in danger of being swamped by a flood of litigation. Professor Harry W. Jones in 1965 told the American Assembly of Columbia University that the judicial system was in deep trouble:

> Twice as many people, therefore twice as many disputes to be settled, twice as many civil claims to be heard, twice as many criminal charges to be tried and determined, but that is by no means the whole story of the law explosion; the full truth is that we have a society that is far more complex and vastly more demanding on law and legal institutions. New rights . . . have been made subject to government regulation and legal contest. New social interests are pressing for recognition in the courts, groups long inarticulate have found legal spokesmen and are asserting grievances long unheard.

Disputes are proliferating, particularly the high-volume type—automobile accident claims, family squabbles, labor grievances, business altercations, claims against massive corporations, and complaints against the government. I shall describe many such controversies in this book. If they all had to be settled in court, a staggering investment would be required to tool up our judicial establishment to handle the case load.

Fortunately, many disputes can be resolved out of court. By negotiation and through the intelligent use of private settlement arrangements, many persons manage to resolve their controversies without burdening the already hard-pressed courts. Some of these techniques are not widely known, though they are practiced by many lawyers and thousands of laymen.

This book will illustrate how ordinary citizens can accomplish it for themselves. These tactical moves are usually based on logic and common sense, but sometimes they require psychological judo. Some techniques can be applied prudently without a lawyer's help; others are extremely hazardous and should be attempted only after the most comprehensive appraisal of legal implications.

Disputes with which I am familiar will be discussed. Each year, thousands of arbitration cases flow through the tribunals of the American Arbitration Association. Those that seem most likely to occur will be described in the hope that the reader, in applying them to similar controversies, may be helped. Where should the reader turn for assistance? How should he use lawyers, and what should he expect of them? The aim here is to provide a practical guide for anyone facing a serious controversy.

We live in a time of rapid change. Our society permits lawful protest, and sometimes concedes to unlawful protest. If this benign climate continues, we shall see increasingly novel grievances asserted in increasingly uncomfortable ways. These demands may test the full limit of our collective patience. There will be a probing for new ways to win contested objectives, including many radical direct action techniques, often necessary to bring the opposing party to the bargaining table.

Techniques used by professional negotiators to expedite settlements will be described in detail. Some of the tactics described may seem harsh or unethical. A word of caution is appropriate. Without restraint, our society would become an inhuman interplay of raw power-equations. It would be customary for clients to demand kickbacks from insurance brokers; for purchasing agents, after forcing maximum price concessions, to require a full measure from the salesman's expense account; and even for influential sponsors to expect compensation from friends helped. If the *quid pro quo* were infinite, the morality of life would suffer. The uncompensated favor would be deemed an eccentricity. Conflict would be played out with a mathematical precision now absent.

In a few businesses, practices may be so venal as to approach this level. Where the bribe and the payoff exist as normal business conduct, the community has already rejected traditional ethical concepts. But most Americans resist the temptation of engaging in unfair practices, and place a high value upon the maintenance of ethical standards. Part of that code is an unwillingness to see the courts used as instruments of unfair coercion.

If this book persuades citizens to relieve our courts of needless litigation, I will be well satisfied. To the extent that controversies can be adjusted privately, the judiciary's current problems may be more easily solved.

Radical and surgical proposals for dealing with faults in our judicial system get serious attention when too many cases have been shoveled through the courthouse door. We see this overburden dramatically when a "crisis in the administration of justice" is caused by riots. In the words of the National Advisory Committee on Civil Disorders:

> Partially paralyzed by decades of neglect, deficient in facilities, procedures and personnel, overwhelmed by the demands of normal operations, some of the nation's lower courts have staggered under the crushing new burdens of civil disorders.

But we also see it when creeping calendar congestion puts back the day of trial until normal civil litigation is rejected in favor of compulsory arbitration, self-help, or deep-seated revulsion against the entire legal system.

The role of the courts should be carefully restricted to prevent their degenerating into pressure cookers for forcing settlements. Bargaining for individual interests should be a private affair. The public can then reserve the specialized apparatus of the courts for more meaningful responsibilities.

Individuals should demand the right to participate directly in their own controversies. The adversary tactics that lead to a lawsuit have sometimes been considered an exclusive arena for those attorneys who are privileged to participate on behalf of clients. The books of Nizer, Liebowitz, Belli, and other articulate raconteurs of courtroom drama show how gratifying such a confrontation can be. Why should the individuals whose interests are involved not also claim the right to handle their own problems if they wish to do so? In many cases there is no legal impediment. Many disputes can be as well handled by the individual disputants as by their representatives.

This is not to say that self-representation is always wise. In complex matters or in litigation, parties are well advised to obtain experienced counsel. But many day-to-day disputes, though serious, are relatively simple and do not involve vital interests or large amounts of money. No one should foreclose himself from deciding whether it is better to go it alone in a particular situation. If one's own efforts fail, one generally can turn the matter over to a lawyer. This book then is written for those who prefer to play the controversy-game themselves, and who would like to know more about its opportunities, dangers, and rules.

Needless to say, the opinions expressed in this book are my own and do not necessarily represent the views of others at the American Arbitration Association. The Association itself is deeply concerned with helping disputants resolve their problems through fair and impartial procedures, but would not necessarily endorse all of the methods for dispute settlement that I shall describe. These are my own views on how to win out of court. I am deeply indebted to the president of the Association, Donald B. Straus, to its directors, and to my associates on the staff for the opportunity that I have enjoyed to study dispute settlement in action and to learn from their combined wisdom.

Discourage litigation. Persuade your neighbors to compromise whenever you can. Point out to them how the nominal winner is often a real loser— in fees, expenses and waste of time.

ABRAHAM LINCOLN

Chapter **1**

THE SECRET COSTS
OF CONFLICT

The average person knows that disputes are likely to arise, and should plan in advance how to deal with trouble, and know where to turn for help.

Safety engineers find it difficult to persuade people to prevent accidents by simply being alert to their origins. In the same way, those of us who concern ourselves with conflict and with how disputes may be resolved find it difficult to alert people to the problems created by conflict, and to get them interested in how conflict might be avoided, or at least controlled.

Is it human nature to shun any thought of trouble? Why do people pretend that their lives will be tranquil? Experience warns us to expect fights. But nevertheless many people plan their lives as if the possibility of future disagreements were nonexistent.

When I practiced law, I saw many clients enter into complex negotiations. They would sign contracts requiring a complicated series of transactions without considering how disagreements might be resolved should any of these arrangements not turn out exactly as planned. Large sums of money would be risked on the basis of a naïve faith in the future. As one particularly imprudent businessman put it, "that's why I hire a lawyer—to do my worrying." By the time he retained a lawyer, this man was deeply in trouble.

Potential disagreement exists in every relationship or transaction, exposing each of us to trouble, unanticipated expense, and the harsh anxieties of litigation. What can we do about it? How can we protect ourselves from the risk of controversy?

This book assumes that each reader will have "A Fight in His Future." Unfortunately, most of us are not able to determine how we will be involved and from which direction attacks will come. No matter how carefully we try to shield ourselves, involvement may be inevitable.

For example, you are waiting for a subway at a crowded station. A train pulls in. The doors open, and you are shoved into the car by the people behind you. In the rush, you are pushed against an old lady, who topples over and is injured. She asks for your name and address. You give them to her. Two months later, you are served with a summons and complaint. She is suing you for $20,000 for personal injuries caused by your negligence. What do you do?

Another example: Your spouse falls in love with a neighbor, locks you out of your house, and retains a lawyer to get her a divorce. Her lawyer informs you that it was your fault. You have been guilty of "cruel and abusive treatment" because you have not given his client enough affection. He demands a great deal of money. When you refuse, you are served with legal process. What do you do?

A third example: You are a manufacturer. You sell your product to a buyer on credit. The price is $2,000. Three weeks later the customer writes to you, claiming that the merchandise was unsuitable. He refuses to pay for it. What do you do?

These are only three of hundreds of situations that any of us might be thrust into unexpectedly, resulting in unwanted conflict and litigation. And always the question arises: What do you do?

First a word of caution: Do not panic. Remember that dispute settlement processes, particularly lawsuits, always move slowly. Never let an opponent rush you, or place you under unnecessary pressure. Resist being put on the defensive.

Asking for help is no disgrace. "Don't keep telling me why I can't do things. If I didn't take chances, my business wouldn't exist." The businessman who uttered these immortal words went bankrupt three years later. He was sued by two customers and a supplier, and accused of tax fraud by the Internal Revenue Service. Protracted litigation, which he could have avoided, destroyed his enterprise.

The Emotional Impact

Even the bickering in a minor dispute can be costly because it distracts the participants from their primary occupation. Don't you find it difficult to return to your work after an argument? Most people do. Your heart is beating more rapidly. You wonder whether you were right. Did you lose your temper? What will your adversary think of you? What will he do? It is not easy to insulate your powers of attention, to concentrate upon your job when you are actively engaged in an important controversy. Arguments exhaust emotional reserves. During an important discord, all other work stops.

In my work we often encounter an individual who has become so engrossed in his case that he is unable to do anything constructive while the matter is pending. Recently, I saw a clear example of this: A middle-aged merchant had sold his neighborhood bookstore to a chain with the understanding that it would gross more than $30,000 each year. The purchaser soon discovered that many of the customers had patronized the shop only because they found it a convenient and pleasant way to spend time with their friend, the owner. When the seller retired, these customers stopped visiting the store and business rapidly declined.

Payment was to be in annual installments over a period of three years. The purchaser claimed that the sales volume of the store had been fraudulently overstated, and refused to pay the second annual installment unless the purchase price was reduced. This simple issue was submitted to arbitration.

What made the case unique was the way it affected the seller. It devastated his normal life. He was unable to look for work. He became preoccupied with the moral implications involved. Had he "cheated" the purchaser? He became obsessed with his "defense." When not discussing the matter with his attorney, he went from store to store in his neighborhood, seeking to justify himself to anyone who would listen. Soon his wife refused to listen. One by one, his neighborhood friends began to avoid him. Increasingly bitter, the claimant awaited the hearing.

Finally the case came to arbitration. The arbitrator made the purchaser pay the second installment, but reduced the purchase price by $3,000. The seller was shocked. He felt he had been "convicted of fraud." He asked me whether he could have the matter reheard. He could not. (Arbitration awards are not subject to appeal.) I advised him to try to forget the case now that it was over. The poor fellow seemed to agree, but it would be a long time before he recovered from his obsessive reaction.

It takes a strong, resilient personality to endure controversy. The ability to regard the contest as if it were happening to someone else is rare.

Professionals learn to do this. No matter how deeply committed a lawyer may become to his client's position, he never forgets that every case has two sides. He insulates himself from emotional involvement. This is a trait worth cultivating.

Shortly after hammering out a new contract with an important employer, a business agent for a militant union of retail clerks was asked whether he was exhausted:

"No. I enjoy bargaining in spite of the hours and the tension. To me, it's a game. I'm too busy planning my moves to become personally involved. Some people allow themselves to get upset. That's a mistake. The negotiator who loses his cool is likely to be rigid, to overlook his opportunities. How effective is a flustered salesman?"

This man is one of the most effective bargainers I have encountered. His skills are not blunted by extraneous emotions. But most of us are uncomfortable when fighting for our rights. We wonder whether our opponent is making a fool of us, feel defensive, and generally grapple with our nerves.

I remember listening to one woman as she entered a courthouse to obtain a contested divorce:

"If there were some way that I could get out of this, I would do it," she told her lawyer. "I felt miserable when I fought my husband at home. To do it in public, with everyone listening to what I say, seems so much worse. I haven't slept for two nights. I couldn't keep anything down this morning. I'm terrified. Get it over with, and get me out of here."

Most people feel that way about going to court. Even when consumed by outrage or by a desire for revenge, they are likely to dread a trial.

Sometimes the lawyer is too concerned with his own part to notice his client. But not always. I know one successful trial lawyer whose secretary goes along to court. Her duty is to stay with the client, to answer questions about the procedure, be reassuring, and to try to reduce the tension in the courtroom.

Even outside the courtroom, controversy is likely to be a source of worry and anxiety. Few people enjoy the prospect of a bitter confrontation with an adversary. For some, it is too harsh a test, for others, too naked an exposure. Some people seek to avoid controversy by making overgenerous concessions or by adopting an arbitrary position. The latter posture often is responsible for escalating a simple disagreement into an impasse, requiring litigation or a needlessly expensive settlement.

For example, a wealthy lady retained a fashionable interior decorator to refurnish her Fifth Avenue apartment. When she discovered discrepancies in the decorator's bill, including a simple error in addition, she refused to pay. The decorator tried to discuss the matter with her, assuming than any differences could be worked out on a rational basis.

The lady was adamant. "Anyone who tries to take advantage of me will have to take the consequences. You were trying to cheat me. I am not going to haggle. If you want to be paid, you will have to sue me." (This sentiment frequently precipitates litigation.)

The decorator considered the prospect of a lawsuit because a lot of money was involved, and he was in need of it. Nevertheless, he decided that it would be better to try to collect his fee some other way. First, he tried sending a polite collection note. The lady sent it back marked "no." Then he asked his aunt, an intimate friend of the lady, to intercede. "I just can't bring myself to sue this woman," he moaned. "And what would my other clients think?"

His aunt was able to persuade her friend that her nephew had simply been careless about the bill. "He is no businessman, my dear, but certainly neither is he a crook." Finally the lady agreed to pay the corrected bill.

The alternative would surely have been a devastating litigation. Fortunately, most people are able to avoid it through negotiation. A friend of mine who was sued recently in the New York Civil Courts, put it this way: "In spite of the fact that I won my case, I will do almost anything to avoid having to go there again. Not only was it the most expensive day of my life, but I felt humiliated every moment I was on the witness stand. I had the feeling that the judge, the jury, and everybody else in the courtroom thought I was lying. How many times in life

do you stand up in front of a man who is being paid to prove
that you are not telling the truth? Only a fool would expose
himself to an unnecessary lawsuit."

Controversies Waste Time

A drawback to litigation is the waste of time involved. Constructive activities have to be postponed. Pleasures and profits
must be held in abeyance. Almost always, your best interests
are served by a prompt resolution of the conflict. And this is
particularly true for those whose time is valuable.

A successful insurance broker bought a brownstone house
in Greenwich Village, planning to convert the lower floors into
a residence and to rent the top two as a luxury apartment. The
building was a rooming house when he bought it. He thought
it would be easy enough to persuade the tenants to move out.
Most of the tenants were willing to move in exchange for payment of their expenses. But not all of them.

A lady tenant who lived in the basement and made her
living there at the "oldest profession" refused to vacate. The
owner spent over a year in court—accumulating lawyer's bills
for $1,200—before he was able to persuade her to quit her
place of business. By the time he obtained full use of the building, all his pleasure in converting it had drained away.

In this man's case, it was fairly simple to calculate exactly
how much time and money was dissipated in this frustrating
and ineffectual litigation. He and his wife told me that they
wasted over two hundred hours on this eviction.

Often, costs are harder to calculate. The general manager
of a manufacturing plant becomes involved in a lawsuit. What
will be the loss to the corporation? The manager might have
been engaged in planning a more efficient operation, but not
while in court. Time must be spent preparing for the trial, and
he will worry about his testimony. Will his word be questioned
during the trial? A plant manager is a sensitive business instrument. His value cannot be calculated in hourly segments. Anxieties created by litigation will affect his performance, destroy
his ability to concentrate, weaken his ability to plan, and poison
his relationships with co-workers. The price of extended litigation can come high. What is true for the business executive and
the corporation is equally true for the individual.

Thus, it is vital that the reader consider whether he can afford a lawsuit which may take several years between the time it is filed and its conclusion. Litigation does not proceed steadily toward a trial. It proceeds spasmodically—the initial threatening letter, the actual filing of the summons and complaint, a demand for more information, interrogatories (formal questions, which must be answered), discovery proceedings, the pretrial hearings in court, where a judge is involved for the first time, and the trial itself. Then for many cases there are appeals.

During this process, crucial procedural motions will have to be decided, each requiring preparation and arguments. At each encounter, attorneys and witnesses will need to review the case. Tactical decisions will have to be made. As the years slip away, the memory of witnesses will erode. Facts will be replaced by memories of facts. By the time the case will be tried, witnesses will not be sure of their memory, suspecting that what they recall is only a recollection of an earlier statement they made years before. Add to the above other worries that surround litigation—fear, nervousness, misunderstanding, and so on—and it is no wonder that people abhor the courts. No wonder most of us are glad to settle our disputes at almost any price.

The businessman is particularly impatient. One recently told me of an interview with his attorney:

"Why can't we settle this case?" he asked.

"We could have settled it earlier. But now it is a leading case in your industry. Everyone is concerned with what the Circuit Court will do. Whatever the decision is, it will influence business decisions in this industry for many years. You have no idea how many calls I get about this case. We are making new law."

"To hell with that. Settle it."

And so it goes. The businessman is more interested in his profits. Like the individual, he has no interest in perfecting the "common law."

The High Cost of Litigation

Litigation has to be expensive because courts try not to make procedural mistakes. Their attempt to achieve procedural perfection causes delay and consequent expense. Anyone who has been involved in litigation will recognize that this is true.

Courts seldom have been adequately financed. Unfortunately, neither salaries nor the other costs of the system are well maintained. The administration of justice deserves more adequate support. There should be more judges, and they should be better paid. In general, the courts should be supplied with more funds and permitted to allocate them more flexibly.

But even if budgetary problems were solved and the most modern administrative procedures were available to the courts, the basic dilemma would still be present because of the protective devices; for example, pre-hearing discovery rules which help the lawyer prepare his case, the complicated rules of trial practice, and the appeal system. While law reformers have narrowed the possibility for procedural mistakes, at the same time they have increased the protective steps that must be taken. This has resulted in further delay, and in more cost to the parties.

As one businessman put it: "My experience with the courts is that they get so involved in providing 'due process' that they often misunderstand the dispute. By the time the lawyers have resolved all the legal niceties, the whole affair is likely to be academic because the parties couldn't wait for a decision, and had to find some other solution to their problem."

He was generalizing. But businessmen often prefer the procedural uncertainties of private settlement techniques to the substantive uncertainties of the courts.

The cost of predictability is high. If the trial lawyer is to come to court armed with complete knowledge of his opponent's case, he must be permitted to examine his opponent's witnesses, as well as to require his opponent's answers to questions. He must be allowed to inspect his opponent's written records. These rights are now a part of modern court procedure.

Lawyers admit that many of these "legal tools" are time consuming and expensive, and sometimes find it hard to justify the high cost of trial preparation. For example, preparing for a small accident case might take fifty hours of the lawyer's time, even though the facts are fairly simple.

Taking depositions of three key witnesses at three hours each	9 hrs.
Preparing and arguing a motion to compel an answer to questions asked	6
Preparing interrogatories	3
Objecting to opponent's of the interrogatories	2
Answering interrogatories (as amended)	10
Arranging for a medical examination	3
Preparing a Motion for Production of a medical report	2
Resisting the opponent's motions to produce	5
Reviewing all the discovery in order to prepare pre-trial memorandum	10

When one realizes that $20 per hour is about the least a lawyer can charge for his time, one will begin to appreciate the costs involved in run-of-the-mill litigation, and this would only reimburse the lawyer for his work on "discovery procedures" involved in one small case.

Sometimes during the discovery process, a fact emerges that so mutilates one party's case that a settlement gushes across the table. Defenders of "full disclosure" base much of their enthusiasm upon such settlements.

It is enough to note that modern pre-trial procedures are expensive and time consuming. They substantially increase the cost to the parties. They create a motivation among laymen to return to less predictable methods for resolving disputes.

But these methods can sometimes be abused by using them as a weapon. Lawyers sometimes force the other party to comply with discovery procedures as a bargaining tool. One Wall Street trial lawyer representing a huge chemical company in a controversy with a supplier of crude oil told me how he expected to settle the case: "We intend to enforce our right to examine every document that has any relevance to this transaction. Over 100,000 separate pieces of paper are involved, and

we will require every one of them. When our opponents realize how disruptive this case is going to be, they will make an
attractive settlement offer. Their company can't afford the expense."

Harassment by legal process is not unknown in individual
disputes. One lady landlord "made the mistake" of reporting a
city building inspector who asked for a bribe. Thirteen violations from three different agencies were issued against her building within four weeks. Here is her description of what followed:

"For several months, the city put me through the mill, first
with one agency, then with another, clearing up violations,
attending departmental hearings, and gradually setting my
house in order."

Fortunately, this woman was a lawyer and could defend
herself. Would she think twice before she reported another
building inspector? "You bet I would."

Infallibility Takes Time

What does it mean in an actual case to avoid procedural
mistakes? If a merchant seeks payment from a buyer in court,
he faces a hazardous course. The very procedural protections
that have been installed to guard the trial against error now
stand in the plaintiff's way as defensive barriers available to
the defendant. Generally, a plaintiff files his case in court by
having his lawyer prepare a detailed complaint, describing the
various facts he will be seeking to prove. The defendant's lawyer files an answer. (Much use is made of forms.) If a technical
error is made in the papers, the other party may have the case
dismissed.

When the matter is properly filed in court, other defensive
opportunities become available to the defendant. As pointed
out earlier, he ordinarily has a right to examine the plaintiff
and the plaintiff's witnesses under oath. He can also require the
plaintiff to answer interrogatories. Court practice may require
that a pre-trial conference be held in court. These demands
must be complied with before the case can be placed on the
calendar for trial.

Even when the preliminary steps have been completed, the
cumbersome procedures required to insure procedural perfection continue to exert their effect on the trial itself. A tran-

script must be made of the proceedings so that both parties will have an opportunity to appeal, possibly claiming that an error was made by the judge or by the other attorney. It is a rare case that does not provide some opportunity for appeal if a losing party is not satisfied by the judgment. In fact, a good trial lawyer can usually create procedural "errors" during the trial to justify an objection and a subsequent appeal. Even the simplest litigation affords opportunities for counsel to obtain procedural advantages, perhaps to vacate the entire proceeding if the result is not satisfactory.

For example, during the trial of a simple negligence case involving an automobile accident, an inexperienced attorney for the plaintiff referred to the defendant's insurance. (The jury is not supposed to know about insurance.) This error permitted the insurance company's lawyer to set aside the verdict, even though no other mistakes occurred during the trial. The plaintiff had to begin all over again.

But suppose the plaintiff wins a judgment. Court systems usually provide one or more levels of appellate review. Decisions reached in the trial court are quite frequently overturned at the first appellate level. And it is not unusual for a higher appellate division to reverse again. All of this, while contributing to the gradual perfection of the "common law," is enormously delaying and creates uncertainty. The participants can be assured that eventually all will be well, and that mistaxes of law will gradually be eliminated. In theory, this may be fine, but in his own case, a party may apprehend a substantial element of gambling, and even if he wins, he may have spent more on legal fees than the case was worth.

The Impact of Litigation on Credit

Remember that your involvement in a lawsuit can affect your reputation and your credit rating. Can you afford that risk?

Even the rumor of a pending lawsuit can impair a company's credit or drive down the value of its stock. For example, *The Wall Street Journal* recently reported that publicity about a multimillion-dollar lawsuit "caused a rout" in one oil company's stock, driving down the price and causing the New York Stock Exchange to stop trading the stock for a day. The lawsuit concerned an alleged agreement by the company to give a New York investment firm a 25 percent working interest in oil concessions in Libya. Although the dispute had simmered for several years, it came to the attention of investors only with the initiation of the lawsuit.

The health of a business depends upon its ability to finance working capital and to obtain adequate credit. Litigation can have a destructive impact. Every business is subject to credit-rating bureau reports, which rely upon consumers, suppliers, or even competitors for sources of information. Naturally, competitors are only too willing to report a company's lawsuit because it immediately reflects upon that company's credit standing. Court dockets are another source of invidious credit information.

The businessman seeks to protect his firm's reputation. To him, the speed with which controversies can be resolved becomes an important consideration. It should also be important to the individual.

One successful executive recently issued instructions that any disagreement with a supplier or a customer was to be brought immediately to his attention. Where his company is wrong, the matter is settled promptly. He feels that this policy alone has improved his company's credit rating.

Before he instituted this policy, many disputes were simply "shelved" by his employees, and it was when confronted with a credit report referring to just such a situation that he decided to install his ironclad rule.

In addition to preventing the case record from becoming public, the private settlement of disputes allows the process of settlement to be accelerated. With litigation, the parties themselves often are powerless to expedite a decision because the courthouse calendar moves at its own pace.

Despite the businessman's eagerness to solve his problems quickly to avoid any damage to his credit standing, a company will sometimes deliberately withhold payment of an outstanding account until necessary capital is available. Business disputes often are the result of a desire to delay payment. This strategy may be a sophisticated method of financing the business, or it may result involuntarily from a general lack of funds. A knowledge of the debtor's situation will often provide a clue.

In a recent case, it became clear that payment on an order of printed fabric was being held up for no other reason than to put pressure on the seller to make good on a further unde-livered order. The buyer admitted that the quality of the first lot was acceptable. As he stated, with some candor: "This guy has left himself wide open to a squeeze. He's short of operating funds—his customers know it. When he's late with an order, his customers naturally apply pressure."

Distracting the Executive's Attention

The issue under dispute is often less important than other things you could be doing. A minor disagreement can distract you from your most important concerns.

A new firm was established to publish technical informa-tion—information which otherwise had to be obtained from dozens of manufacturers' catalogs—on components used in the electronics industry. The officers and employees of the com-pany seemed well qualified to produce the product and to sell it. The price for the service seemed reasonable. The budget was prudently designed in the light of probable costs and an-ticipated revenue. The investors believed that every eventuality had been considered, and that the operation was sure to make money.

They were wrong. The business failed. Two vice presi-dents, one in charge of production, the other in charge of sales, were responsible for the failure. Whatever one attempted, the other would balk. They disagreed at every turn. When they were not actively fighting over the management of the corpora-tion, they would be sulking in their offices. Other executives, who could view the situation objectively, saw that the conflict was destroying any prospects the corporation might have had. But the two adversaries, locked in their private battle for con-trol of the small company, were unwilling to resolve their dif-ferences. Month after month the unsatisfactory condition con-tinued. It hamstrung the operation of the business. Production was delayed because they were in disagreement over a particular format. Sales were held back and renewals were prejudiced be-cause delivery could not be made on subscriptions.

The outside directors called a crisis meeting. They delivered an ultimatum. One of the men would have to leave the business. An all-night session ensued. The chairman tried to conciliate, first talking with one partner, and then the other. No compromise could be reached. In the early morning, he gave up, telling the partners that he was abandoning his attempt, and went home.

The following day, the production manager locked his rival out of the premises. For three days the stalemate continued. Finally the largest creditor of the company was able to convince the partners that the business was doomed unless the impasse could be resolved. Once again negotiations began. It took two weeks before a satisfactory arrangement could be reached; the marketing director would leave the business in exchange for promissory notes and nonvoting stock. Only the personal guarantee of one of the outside directors made it possible for the corporation to continue in operation.

When the directors reviewed the net effect of this pointless quarrel between two otherwise well-motivated business partners, they agreed that the event had retarded the growth of the company by at least six months. In fact, the quarrel delivered a fatal blow to the enterprise; it never recovered. Within months, the remaining partner resigned, selling his interest to an outsider.

A Positive Point of View

It is intelligent to try to handle disputes promptly and efficiently and to look upon controversies as a kind of problem, an adversary problem.

Many top executives of the largest and most successful national corporations state that it is the policy of their companies to resolve every dispute as promptly as possible. They avoid litigation. They avoid arbitration. They even avoid prolonged negotiation. Wherever possible, they carefully study the facts of a situation and then make a liberal but final offer to the other party, sometimes advising him that if their offer is not accepted, they will eliminate him from their list of suppliers. Where a corporation has enough power to make good its threat, this policy works. It resolves disputes promptly. It is a positive approach.

A businessman who discovers that a firm with whom he deals is a frequent source of controversy will stop doing business with that firm. A businessman who learns that one of his employees is creating disagreements with his co-workers or with outside people, will rid his business of that employee. Certain persons are trouble breeders. In many industries, they become known. They should be avoided.

This tendency can be overemphasized. I know of one industry in which even legitimate claims are apt to be withdrawn because these companies are overly sensitive about their reputation. As the owner of one company told me: "My competition watch like hawks. If we sue anyone, they broadcast the news, trying to make it look as if we are litigation hungry. We can't afford to give our competition ammunition. So when we're rebuffed, we write off the claim, charging it to customer relations."

In such industries, firms attempt to obtain payment in advance. Where cash payment is not practical and claims are apt to arise, some private system of dispute settlement may become particularly appealing.

This can work out quite well, as in the case where a large number of blank airline tickets were stolen from a travel agency and successfully presented for refund at an airline desk. Was the loss the fault of the travel agency or of the airline? A private arbitration as to which of them should bear the loss was not even reported in the trade press. Publicity could have proved embarrassing to both businesses.

The prudent businessman knows that unexpected contingencies may arise, and tries to guard against them. An individual should do the same thing. Often it is possible to insure against legal exposure, as well as the responsibility of defending a lawsuit. This is done in the ordinary automobile insurance policy. Here the policyholder protects himself against liability, and obtains free legal representation in the event he is sued.

For example, with typical coverage, if you have an accident that causes injuries to another driver, you are likely to be sued by him. When you are served with legal papers, charging that your carelessness caused the accident, you need only notify your insurance company. A lawyer will be assigned to defend you. The negotiations with the attorney for the other driver will be handled by your insurance company.

To the extent that you are able to forecast the kinds of disputes likely to arise, it is then possible to guard against them. And a good lawyer or insurance broker will help you check off your most likely exposures, and will advise you how they can be reduced or insured against.

HOW TO USE LEGAL
FIRE POWER

Lawyers often are asked to take the conflict load off the shoulders of their clients. There may be times when it will be wiser to handle a dispute yourself. But you should know when to turn to a lawyer and how to select the right one.

Lawyers have many uses. They serve as advisers regarding legal rights and obligations of the parties, as guides to complicated legal procedures, and as manipulators of the voluminous paper work that has become so fashionable in our documentary society. But since this book concentrates upon conflict, I will focus upon the part of the lawyer's job that involves fighting for his client.

Because a good lawyer is a good weapon, the mere threat of retaining a particular firm or lawyer may work wonders: "My law firm is [well-respected name]. If you and I don't come to a prompt agreement, I'm going to see them tomorrow."

"If you don't want me to bring in [prestigious lawyer], you had better make up your mind to be reasonable."

To your opponent, the bringing in of a lawyer means a lawsuit, inevitable expenses, and additional anguish. No wonder this threat is often effective.

Selecting the Right Lawyer

If you decide that you need a lawyer, be careful to select one who specializes in the kind of case that is involved, and who has a strong reputation in the community.

Remember that there are many specialized kinds of attorneys. If you get the wrong one, he may be completely unqualified to handle your particular problem.

The executive secretary of a state bar association puts it this way: "It is not that most of our lawyers are not well equipped to give good legal service. The real problem is that clients ask them to do jobs outside their area of knowledge. When you tell a corporate lawyer to operate in Magistrate's Court, you are not very likely to get good results. Too many lawyers try to operate outside of their specialties."

Notwithstanding, traditionally attorneys have claimed an ability to advise clients about most areas of the law, and have resented any implication that their activity should be restricted to narrow fields. Specialization is still being debated within the organized bar, but local bar associations normally prohibit attorneys from advertising their specialized fields of activity to the public.

Where does this leave you in obtaining expert advice in a dispute? In each community, with a little research, you can find out who the good lawyers are for particular types of problems. If people spent as much time selecting their lawyers as they spend picking out their new automobiles, the legal profession would have few public relation problems.

Help in selecting a lawyer is available from bar associations, banks, title companies, real estate brokers, and other organizations whose staffs have acquired a working knowledge of their fields. You may be tempted to seek legal information as well. Sometimes a lay specialist may be more expert than a lawyer, particularly where the lawyer is not a specialist. At other times the advice given by such organizations is tainted by self-interest and may plunge you into unexpected legal difficulties. Then, independent legal advice would have been a good investment.

It is unwise to place complete faith in the recommendations of any one source. It is prudent to obtain several recommendations. In a small community, this can be done easily. In a larger city, it may be harder because there are so many lawyers.

On the other hand, in the big cities large law partnerships exist with experts in most fields. If the partner originally contacted is the wrong one, he will provide an appropriate man within his partnership. Some smaller firms maintain similar relationships with outside experts in specialties that they themselves do not handle. For example, some firms do not handle marital cases. When a client comes to them for this kind of service, they will recommend a specialist.

Mere expertise is not the sole test. You want a lawyer who is most likely to help you win. Since nine out of ten disputes are resolved through bargaining, it is only common sense to retain a lawyer who is a hard negotiator, a man known for his intractable perseverance, his willingness to unleash unlimited legal fire power, and for his far-reaching demands. In bargaining, nice guys finish last.

A friend of mine recently went through a difficult and expensive divorce proceeding. He put it this way: "When I asked around for a lawyer to represent me, I was given two choices. One was called the worst son-of-a-bitch in the profession. The other was recommended to be highly qualified and completely reliable. I picked the wrong lawyer. My wife retained the son-of-a-bitch. I will be regretting my choice for years."

Lawyers should not be picked on the basis of their personal charm. They should be pulled off the rack with the same objectivity with which a big-game hunter selects a rifle.

What Should the Lawyer Be Asked to Do?

The client should be certain what he wants his lawyer to do. This itself can be a source of controversy. The relationship between client and attorney is truly effective only when both clearly understand their obligations. But how can a client be certain that his lawyer will do the job he wants done?

It is sensible to discuss the case thoroughly before any legal work begins. The client is naturally familiar with the circumstances contributing to the problem. He should take the time to describe the situation in detail, and be clear about his instructions. Is the lawyer being asked to advise the client about his legal rights and obligations? Or is he also being asked to do something? This is entirely up to the client. He can put any limitation upon legal services.

Where the role of the lawyer is not clearly identified and understood, there is a possibility of conflict. The client may come to believe that his attorney is taking over the case—a common complaint. A client often grumbles that when he places his case in the hands of an attorney he loses control of it. It is usually his own fault. Lawyers must follow instructions. It is up to the client to express any limitations clearly and to define the area of responsibility for each. Otherwise, he should accept the risk of his lawyer acting on his own.

A lawyer often has difficulty understanding exactly what his client expects of him. A young lawyer was told by his client, the owner of a fashionable New York City town house, that the gutter on an adjoining building was overflowing into his garden. "What are my rights?" The client inquired on the telephone.

The attorney did not know. Being conscientious, he went to the firm's library and read the law. Several days later, he called his client and quoted chapter and verse exactly what his legal remedies would be in order to protect himself from the troublesome splatter of the drainpipe.

"Oh!" said the client. "I didn't expect you to do any research. I just wanted to know what arguments to use when I called my neighbor. Anyway, everything is settled. The gutter was fixed."

That client did not want an accurate opinion. He merely needed ammunition for threatening his neighbor in an effort to persuade him to repair the drainpipe. All too frequently attorneys believe that they are being asked to provide definitive answers when a client only requires an off-the-cuff opinion.

The most violent complaints about lawyers' fees are usually caused by the fact that the client was not told in advance how much work the lawyer would have to do. The attorney is seldom able to estimate how comprehensive his research will have to be. A perfunctory search of the authorities may result in error. As research continues, the risk grows slighter. When should the search be terminated? When do economic factors impinge upon perfection? These are the considerations that confront an attorney when he is asked to estimate the cost of his advice on a complex subject. If he guesses too low, his client is in for a surprise when he gets the bill. Nevertheless, the client should inquire.

Much of the attorney's work is done out of his client's sight. He may spend hours reading cases and statutes. The client does not see this. He is aware only of advice that results. This too is a potential source of conflict between client and attorney.

There are a few things for a client to guard against. His lawyer should not be allowed to take too legalistic an approach, overlooking some of the practical considerations. And particularly when the lawyer wants to invest his time in contesting a procedural point or take an expensive appeal, a client has a right to be sure that there is enough at stake to justify the additional cost and delay. The lawyer's intellectual interest in avoiding and correcting legal errors in the courts does not coincide with a client's interests, which may be somewhat more practical. But it should be recognized that the threat of an appeal, or of litigation generally, can often be used by lawyers to force further concessions from an opponent. Just because needless litigation should be avoided does not mean that a client should restrain his attorney from threatening to sue.

One of New York's best known trial lawyers recently told me about a case that will illustrate an exception to the rule that most people should avoid litigation. He and his wife are art collectors. One Saturday morning at a new gallery, they discovered a painting by a French impressionist, which both of them liked. The lawyer asked the young salesgirl whether the painting was available. She assured them that it was and told him the price. It was high but within his means. After conferring briefly with his wife, he agreed to buy the picture and asked the salesgirl to have it delivered to his house on the following Monday.

When he and his wife returned to their apartment after a leisurely lunch at a nearby restaurant, they received a telephone call.

"I am the owner of the gallery you visited this morning. I am terribly sorry, sir. A mistake was made by my assistant. In fact, I had given an option on the picture you admired to a customer who has bought many of my paintings. I had given him until one o'clock. Only fifteen or twenty minutes after you left my gallery, my customer called and agreed to take the painting at my asking price. I am particularly sorry because I was told by my assistant how much you and your wife liked the painting. But you will understand that I had given my word in advance and that this purchaser has a prior right to yours."

"I am afraid you are quite wrong," the lawyer said. "Your assistant told me nothing about any option on the picture. In fact she said it was available for sale. She quoted me a price, we discussed the terms, I agreed to buy it. I am the owner of the picture."

"I am sorry to say that my assistant knew nothing about the option. Nevertheless, the option existed and I am bound by it."

"That's your problem. I expect my painting on Monday morning. If you do not deliver that picture to my apartment, I will be forced to bring a legal action against your gallery to obtain possession of my property."

"I do not care to argue with you. I have made my position absolutely plain. You are being extremely unfair. I had already promised it to another. He has purchased it."

"I should tell you perhaps that I am a partner in the law firm of [he named a large well-known law firm]. I specialize in litigation. Nothing would please me more than an opportunity to take this matter to court. I promise you that unless I have my picture on Monday morning, I will sue you and your gallery and will obtain a court order awarding me the picture in addition to other expenses which you will have caused me."

The owner of the gallery hung up. The picture was not delivered on the following Monday. Without further ado, the lawyer told one of the young men in his office to prepare a summons and complaint to obtain possession of the picture and to collect damages for its nondelivery. The papers were served on the following Wednesday. On Thursday, the gallery owner called the lawyer at his office.

"I don't know why you are persecuting me," he said. "I think you are being extremely nasty. It is the first time that this has ever happened to me or my gallery. Ordinarily, people I do business with lean over backward to be ethical. But knowing you are a lawyer, I know that you are in a position to harass me in the courts. I have had to call my customer in St. Louis and plead with him to release me from my bargain—I told him how unfairly you were treating me. I will have your picture delivered tomorrow. I hope you are satisfied."

"Thank you," the lawyer said. "I think you are being very wise. I have studied the legal rights of this matter and I can assure you that the ownership of the picture is mine. I will expect it tomorrow."

Sometime after the picture was delivered, I happened to

see it in the lawyer's home, during a cocktail party. When I admired it, he told me the whole story. "Would you have sued the man to a conclusion?" I asked.

"Probably not. But it was easy enough to have the papers prepared, and to serve them. Once he learned who I was and realized that I would not hesitate to drag him into court, I expected him to cave in. As it turned out, I was correct in my judgment."

"But what if this man had retained a lawyer to represent him in court? What if the buyer in St. Louis had refused to release the painting and had forced the gallery owner to send it to him?"

"Then I would probably have conceded the painting. It would have been difficult to obtain possession of the painting in court. And I knew that it would not be easy for me to prove damages. But I had impressed the gallery owner as a hard-nosed, stubborn person. With that background, I thought he might fall for my bluff. Thank goodness he did. And it is a lovely painting, isn't it?"

Surveys of the legal profession disclose that a common complaint made by clients is delay in processing cases. (As we have seen, there is not much the individual lawyer can do about speeding a case through the courts.) Some of the dissatisfaction is caused by the lawyer's failure to tell his client about probable delays, why they exist, and how long they may be expected to last. In other cases, delay may be caused by the lawyer himself, but here it should not be tolerated.

A client has a right to ask his lawyer what progress is being made on the case. Unfortunately, many laymen simply assume that years will elapse before their claims will be decided. Sometimes, a lazy lawyer will simply put the file aside and forget about it.

In one case, many months went by before the client bothered to ask about his case. The lawyer told him that the delay was caused by "court congestion." In fact, he had not even bothered to file the case in court. Almost a year later, the client again got around to asking for a progress report. The lawyer said that the matter was "in negotiation." He had not even contacted the other party. Somehow the client found out, and began to worry. He called the Grievance Committee of the Bar

Association. When the attorney for the Grievance Committee
approached the lawyer, he said he had lost the file. But when
the Bar Association persevered, all the facts came out. Fortunately for the client, his lawyer's negligence was exposed
before the time limit had run out on his claim. Another lawyer
was able to file the case and obtain a recovery. The first lawyer
was disbarred.

Such flagrant malpractice is rare. But no matter how meticulously most lawyers carry out their duties, they all operate
under various pressures. They are not able to process each
case as quickly as a client would like. It is sensible for a client
to request progress reports from his attorney, if only to show
his interest in the matter.

Ordinarily, lawyers appreciate this. As one highly respected
corporate attorney put it, "I like it when a client calls to find
out what's happened. It gives me an opportunity to keep him in
the picture. It also enables me to explain the tactical moves I
am making in his behalf, to firm up my contact with him, and
also to find out if there have been any new developments in
the case from the business side."

Many malpractice charges against lawyers could have been
avoided if the client had checked up on his attorney more often.
The lawyer is working for the client, and should be given
adequate supervision. The client should know what is being
accomplished on his case. He should feel free to request estimates of legal fees and costs, as well as an estimated timetable.
The right to question his lawyer's judgment or to handle the
matter in some different way should never be compromised.

Sometimes, rather than ask his own attorney about his
case, a client will call other lawyers for informal opinions on
whether the dispute is being handled properly. This is probably
a mistake. A lawyer will hesitate to criticize what another lawyer
is doing. And no responsible attorney would give legal advice
on the basis of a casual and probably inaccurate description of
the facts.

Where a client has selected the wrong attorney, he can
always obtain a replacement. This switch should not be made
too often. In a small community, a "lawyer-hopping" client
may find it difficult to retain competent counsel.

One such fellow was a Hungarian who claimed to have inherited substantial contract claims against British and American

manufacturing corporations. According to him, these companies had taken orders for machinery purchased for his father's industrial plants. He produced voluminous correspondence, order forms, and affidavits "proving" the validity of his position. I spent several weekends trying to piece together his evidence. One Saturday afternoon, while rummaging through his file cabinets (in a dusty warehouse in a remote part of the Bronx), I came upon correspondence with a dozen leading law firms. This man had gone to each of them, persuaded each to look into his case, and when told that the claim was groundless, had moved on to another. After discovering this evidence of "lawyer-hopping," I put on my coat, shut my briefcase, and went home, wiser and far less trusting.

Often a client will ask his attorney to do something he himself is reluctant to do. People are greedy at times, and can be cruel and overreaching. We tend to overlook our own mean and disagreeable characteristics. But when we hire a lawyer, we may expect him to represent these same instincts. A client may ask his lawyer to threaten, to make unfair demands, and to play the villain.

It is the lawyer who is expected to wear the "black hat." But the client will play the role of the good guy, making concessions, tempering harsh demands with equity, portraying the rational, understanding conciliator who makes settlement possible. How often does this occur?

One client was very frank about it. He retained a young lawyer to collect a delinquent account in an industry not noted for its charity. His instructions were to go in "like a tiger," threaten everything and anything. If the attorney was successful, the client hinted, "more compatible" legal work would follow. One morning, unannounced, the lawyer charged into the debtor's office, armed with a summons and complaint, and threw himself into the role. When he had completed his act, threatening and blustering, the debtor was surely convinced that he was dealing with a malignant and implacable eccentric.

The following day, the client called his debtor and offered to settle the claim at a reasonable discount. The offer was promptly accepted. The client informed the attorney that he had been agreeably surprised by the change in the man's point of view.

Similar techniques are used widely by businessmen to collect debts. The system works much like an artillery barrage. The lawyer presents a hard, unconciliatory posture. Then the client capitalizes on the shock value by offering his opponent an unexpected and welcome bargain. Accurate timing is essential.

Sometimes a client's use of his attorney depends upon the innocence of the victim. Many people experience acute anxiety when approached by a hostile lawyer bristling with demands. It takes insouciance to say, "So sue me!"

The hard-line negotiating stance is particularly effective in matrimonial matters, where the lawyer may be dealing with an unsophisticated and disturbed housewife. Sometimes he will believe that his appropriate role is to scare the other party by filing suit, by threatening custody proceedings, or by taking any one of the harsh legal steps that are available in domestic litigation. This approach can be extremely effective against a guilty spouse, or against a more conciliatory attorney. But where both attorneys adopt this stance, they may escalate an issue into a vicious court battle that will leave scars and debts long after the case has been resolved.

A Choice of Remedies

Don't let anyone tell you that you have no choice of remedies. It is your dispute. Ordinarily, there are no restrictions as to how you may handle it. You are not required to proceed in the traditional methods. Since your own interests are involved, you have a right to make concessions or to gamble.

In dispute settlement every alternative is risky—litigation, arbitration, even settlement discussions. For example, if an adversary is obstinate, or hopelessly entrenched in his position, he is likely to refuse to make concessions. By letting him know you are willing to negotiate, you may weaken your position and invite crushing defensive measures that your adversary would not otherwise have used. There is risk in every choice. You must appraise each of your options carefully to decide which is most appealing for the particular case.

Here, attorneys can be useful. The daily activities of a busy practitioner provide constant exposure to conflict experiences, which help a lawyer understand the odds. Not always.

The mere fact that a man is an attorney is no guarantee that he knows how to handle disputes. The law may be a minor part of the problem.

A businessman, on the other hand, may negotiate constantly, and be skilled in the art. Often he is endowed with sharper negotiating skills than his legal adviser. A recent study by a research team of the Harvard Business School confirmed the fact that many businessmen demand a strong voice in dispute settlement. Particularly where a disagreement turns on a knowledge of industry practices, it seems sensible for businessmen to claim this right.

An inexperienced attorney representing a dress manufacturer was offered the choice of taking back merchandise or being paid a small sum of damages. He accepted the first option without bothering to ask his client. To his dismay, he discovered that because the fad for the garments had vanished, they were almost worthless. The client would have been glad to accept any sum so long as he did not have to take back the garments. This attorney should have checked with his client.

"Look, Charlie," the client warned him. "It took me thirty years to learn this business. I don't hire a lawyer to tell me what my garments should sell for. Let me handle that part, okay?"

As for gambling, a good example is the situation of a young labor lawyer who was having difficulty collecting a legal fee from a small local union. He had given an estimate for preparing and handling a case before the National Labor Relations Board. But his work had involved more legal research than he had anticipated. His bill exceeded the estimate. The business agent would not pay.

The lawyer had an appointment that afternoon to discuss the matter. He was afraid that the union would stop using him as its attorney. The business agent was a rough-cut diamond, and a harsh negotiator. I knew that he loved to gamble.

"Why don't you flip a coin?" I asked my friend.

"Be serious," he replied. "This is important to me."

"It might work. I know this guy."

"I know him too. That's what worries me. I can't haggle with him. If I push him too far, I'll lose my client. But you may be right. If he loses on a gamble, he won't resent it."

That afternoon, my friend followed my suggestion and
lost. He still represents the union and has received many times
more in legal fees than the original amount involved. This was
one dispute that could not have been resolved in court for
very practical reasons. A lawsuit would have ended this lawyer's
labor career. And he would have lost face with the business
agent if he had backed down. A toss of the coin was a practical
solution. When an opponent is a "gambling man," the flip of
coin may be a useful option. If the union leader had been less
powerful or if more money had been in dispute, some other
option might have been more attractive.

The Lawyer as an Innovator

A business lawyer carefully described the various ways his
client might collect from a delinquent purchaser. He explained
that it would be possible for a case to be filed in a state court.
Or it might be preferable, he said, to consider the federal court.
He explained the differences between the two court systems
and the advantages and disadvantages of each. And he added
that another alternative would be to agree with the other party
to arbitrate.

"What!" said the client. "You mean I don't have to go to
court!"

Relatively very few cases end up in court. Lawyers resolve
most contested matters through settlement discussions. More
often than not, a suit is filed in court only for psychological
reasons to force the other party to compromise. Settlement
sometimes results though often a lawsuit can have the opposite
effect. Attitudes may harden, and the defendant may call in
an attorney.

Because of such working experience, many lawyers have
become expert at helping clients resolve disputes out of court.
They try to find practical, useful solutions. They are professional problem-solvers looking for ways to increase their "productivity" and to close files crisply to the satisfaction of their
clients. This is an important part of their service, worth looking
into.

However, a sophisticated defendant will realize that courts
afford opportunities for delay. But it can be expensive to press
litigation to a successful conclusion. Sometimes it is unavoid-

able. One impatient woman could not understand why her divorce would have to be handled in court under New York's State law. "Look! It's my problem! Why do I have to wait for the courts to handle it in some silly, old-fashioned way? Why can't George and I work out our own deal? Then the judge can put his rubber stamp on it." For divorce actions and a few other situations, the courts are an exclusive forum. But in most disputes between private parties, the government does not involve itself in settlement discussions, or require that cases be resolved in court.

Some lawyers hesitate to depart from traditional methods of litigation. This would be expected. But many are excellent innovators, understand their adversaries, the available options, and the pace and normal agenda for negotiating sessions. They understand the dynamics of dispute settlement, and are able to manipulate the process.

"In bargaining," an elderly judge told me, "the important factor is initiative. I spend much of my time watching lawyers bargain for their clients. In my experience, the most effective lawyers bargain aggressively with a positive plan of action. They make the other lawyer play the game on their terms."

For example, a lawyer may advise his client that a decision should be reached quickly. A manufacturer of print fabric had sued a textile jobber to recover payment on an order that the jobber claimed to be substandard. The jobber had been about to transfer the management of his business to his son-in-law so that he could retire to Florida. But he was the only one personally familiar with the contract and with the quality of the material. He asked his attorney what he should do about the lawsuit.

If the case were allowed to languish in court, the attorney argued, it would plague the firm for many years. It would be better if this relatively insignificant dispute (the case involved $30,000) could be closed out before the business was transferred. The other party would be delighted to have the matter adjusted.

The matter was withdrawn from court, promptly arbitrated before a panel of textile experts, and a partial recovery was awarded to the manufacturer. Within three months, the jobber was able to transfer the business to his son-in-law with no outstanding lawsuits.

There are many reasons why it may be in the interest of all sides to have a controversy disposed of promptly. Naturally when a business is to be sold, it is prudent to resolve all outstanding claims promptly. When tax liability must be fixed in a certain fiscal year or when a gain or loss must be allocated to a particular period, businessmen often desire prompt determination. Practical reasons are usually persuasive. Then if it is desirable that the matter proceed swiftly, an attorney can be expected to design procedures to bring about desired results.

In one arbitration case, the president of the claimant company agreed in advance with his lawyer that they had a weak case and should seek every opportunity to settle differences during the arbitration proceedings. They agreed on a procedure. The primary task of the president would be to find an opportunity to talk settlement with the other party. The lawyer would handle the arbitration hearing, itself.

The president knew that his opponent, the purchasing agent for a textile mill, was very nervous about testifying. He would be the final witness for the defense.

As the time for him to testify approached, the purchasing agent became visibly upset. While the next-to-last witness was answering a few final questions, the purchasing agent left the hearing room, followed by the president seconds later. After a few minutes, the questioning of all witnesses was completed, and the hearing came to a standstill.

At this point, the attorney for the claimant, guessing that an important conversation might be going on in the men's room, in the interest of stalling, asked the arbitrator for permission to raise a point of procedure. He argued that briefs should not be filed until a complete transcript of the evidence had been approved by both parties. He then described the points that he intended to raise in his brief, and continued to filibuster on the subject for a full twenty minutes. Opposing counsel, unaware of the important conference taking place elsewhere, joined in the debate. The clock ticked on. The arbitrator listened patiently, permitting both lawyers to talk until they had completely explored the subject. The tribunal administrator attending the hearing reported to me later that he could not understand why both counsel wasted the arbitrator's time over such a trivial issue.

The moving attorney, at his wit's end, stalling for more

time, asked the tribunal administrator to check the exhibits to see whether they had been properly marked. The administrator methodically checked through the exhibits while the lawyer nervously watched the clock.

His efforts were finally rewarded when the two principals returned to the hearing room and announced that the case had been settled.

The president of the claimant company had followed a basic rule. He had pressed for a settlement at a time when his opponent was under personal pressure to resolve the case.

The managing partner of a large Boston law firm feels this way about innovation: "My problem is maximizing professional effort. I must persuade my senior lawyers to "kick" their old-fashioned methods. The younger men have to be protected. Otherwise they do clerical work. Too many firms permit their lawyers to waste their time on inefficient work practices. Any big firm that doesn't have a full-time administrator is mismanaging this function."

When I asked him whether litigation presented his firm with a particular problem, he answered this way: "Sure, when my lawyers spend a day in court, they are often wasting their time. They sit around, waiting for their cases to be called, reading and gossiping. At the end of the day, they have not accomplished much for our clients or for the firm."

At each partners' meeting in this law firm, a list of the outstanding cases is reviewed, beginning with the case that has been with the firm the longest and ending with the most recent. The partner responsible reports on the posture of each case. The other partners ask questions and make suggestions as to how the matter might be more promptly resolved. Quite frequently, these sessions result in settlements.

In one recent case, the firm's client was a machinery manufacturer seeking to recover damages from an out-of-state public utility. The partner in charge of the litigation described the issue: a refusal to pay for some machinery on the basis that it was not up to specifications. One of the partners happened to remember that the president of the utility company had roomed with the executive vice president of the client at college.

"Would it be a good idea for me to discuss this matter

with my friend the executive vice president and remind him that his roommate is involved?"

"It sure would," the litigating partner said. "This will be a hard case for me to win. There was something wrong with the machinery. We have had technical problems with this model before. Other customers have refused to pay until we offered a price concession."

A phone conversation between the former roommates disposed of the matter. When the president of the utility company interceded with his purchasing department, the matter was satisfactorily resolved. The client was quite pleased that the matter had been brought to his attention.

"We expected that matter to drag on for years," the executive vice president later told one of the partners. "Usually, when a matter has to be turned over to an outside attorney, we simply resign ourselves to infinite delay. You fellows did us a service by bringing me back into the picture. We obtained a satisfactory result and did it quickly. Congratulations."

The Lawyer's Duty to Perfect the Law

Be sure that the steps taken by your lawyer are clearly in your interest. At a bar association meeting, one may hear an attorney say that a lower court decision was wrong, that he would like to appeal it in order to perfect the law on the point, but that he is unable to persuade his client to take an appeal. This dialogue occurs so frequently that it must be a source of continuous misunderstanding between lawyers and clients. The lawyer has a problem. He owes his primary duty to his clients. But he also has a duty to the law. He seeks to eliminate procedural errors in the cases he handles, otherwise they may become embedded in the law and provide a possible source of error in future cases. These errors may seem unimportant to his client because they may have little economic impact.

Such an underlying conflict is not present in every case. But it arises frequently enough so that clients should be aware of it and guard themselves against the increased expense of being asked to correct such errors. "What is it worth to me?" they should ask. Unless the lawyer can give them a satisfactory answer, they should abandon the case—leaving the lawyer unrequited.

Justice loses its value when it seems too expensive or when it delays too long the final resolution of the client's problem. This is basic.

As one lawyer recently remarked at an arbitration seminar, "Don't think for a minute that your clients are genuinely interested in being right, or in seeing justice prevail. They couldn't care less about justice; they only want to win."

But many lawyers are too committed to the ideals of their profession not to yearn as well for justice. This interest of the lawyer does sometimes result in the client being persuaded to spend more in legal fees than the resolution of the issue is worth. In one case involving about $6,000, the outcome was not particularly significant to either party. But both attorneys urged their clients to appeal a procedural ruling by the trial judge because they felt it was bad law and that they had an obligation to have it corrected.

In the end, the combined legal fees were only a few hundred dollars less than the total amount in dispute. As one of the clients told me later, "We were fools to go ahead with it. I had no idea that the fees were going to be so high. For one thing, since it was the lawyers who wanted to appeal the case, I thought that they would reduce their charges. No such luck. Legal expenses like these have persuaded me that a man's a fool to go to court."

And it is such cases that have produced such popular definitions of the lawyer, as "a man who induces two other men to take off their jackets and fight, and then runs away with their jackets"; or "a fellow who is willing to spend your last dollar to prove that he is right"; or "the friend who rescues your business from its enemies and keeps it for himself."

The Use of House Counsel

The increasing use by corporations of inside counsel should be borne in mind by individuals who deal with corporations against which they have disputes. Some large corporations have hundreds of these lawyers on their staffs. Often these men are specialists—in tax counseling, labor relations, or international law.

One case indicates that there may be significant differences between them and outside attorneys.

A franchised location for selling ice cream was eliminated when a major highway was redirected to a new location. The owner of the property wanted to relocate his restaurant on the same highway. He first approached the franchise company's law firm, and explained his problem to one of the partners.

"Absolutely not," the lawyer said. "I drew up those contracts myself. We have no obligation to give you another location. Your franchise was limited to the one place."

Dismayed by the attorney's attitude, the former franchise holder went to the franchise company and talked to the head of the legal department. Here he got a different reception. This lawyer knew that his company had profited from the man's former operation. He recognized the advantages of putting him back in business. He was less concerned with what the contract required.

"We have another franchise holder located ten miles down the road from the spot you are after. Let's see if we can't get him to agree to let you relocate. Maybe a small payment would make it worth his while. Anyway, I don't think you'd be competing very much. Let me try to work it out. You are the kind of franchise operator this company needs. I think we ought to try to help you solve your problem."

The man complained about the treatment he had received from the outside attorney. He was quite angry. "Lucky I didn't take his advice," he said.

The inside lawyer laughed and said, "Oh, well, we just use that law firm when we want to discourage people."

The dispute was resolved through the good offices of the general counsel of the company. In return for a $2,000 payment, the owner of the franchise down the road gave permission for a new location. The payment was absorbed equally by the company and the franchise operator.

Chapter 3

FORCING A FAIR
SETTLEMENT

Well-recognized techniques can be used successfully by individuals to force fair settlements of disputes. Although there is a wealth of potential controversies likely to pounce upon each of us without notice, ranging from haggling about the price of merchandise to the most complicated negotiation over the sale of a business, the principles of bargaining can be applicable to all.

The first thing to decide is how to begin bargaining with your opponent. Be careful not to do this in a way that weakens your position. On the other hand, avoid an opening move that escalates the dispute into an action in court.

This is a particularly sensitive point in the resolution process because it may fix your subsequent relationship, lending it a conciliatory tone or an atmosphere of militancy.

"The first phone call is the crucial point," one business lawyer warned. "After I hang up I almost always know whether or not litigation is going to be necessary. There should be nothing casual about that important first contact." Deciding with whom it will be best to deal can also be a critical step in the bargaining process.

"People have different breaking points. By the time I have sized up my opposition, I have picked the man who seems most amenable to compromise. I go for him." This, from the spokesman of a union bargaining team.

Once you know your adversary, you can plan the scenario which you hope will lead to success, the diplomacy, tactics, and probable concessions that you will have to make. These will depend upon an accurate understanding of the dispute, the reasons why it had to arise, and the best formula for obtaining a successful result.

As a negotiator, you should be able to use the customary techniques for forcing concessions that are described in this chapter with examples of how they can be applied. When should direct pressure be placed upon an adversary? When is it appropriate to involve some third party or government agency in an attempt to escalate pressure for settlement? When would a mediator serve a useful purpose? By learning how to use such skills you can make yourself better equipped for obtaining advantages from the bargaining process. Much will depend upon your force of character, persuasiveness, power to present an articulate case, and even your economic strength. But if the principles are understood, much can be made of very little. Like David against Goliath, a skillful and aggressive individual can topple the most powerful institution.

How to Start the Bargaining

It is not always feasible to pick up a telephone and ask your opponent to bargain. Often your opponent will decide that he has nothing to gain from discussing the matter, because he would prefer the situation to stay exactly as it is. When the other fellow owes you money, he may not be at all enthusiatstic about discussing how much he owes, or when he will pay you. You may have to take action to convince him that you mean business and to start him thinking seriously about your claim.

The filing of a court action is sometimes used by an attorney to shock an opponent into good faith negotiations. Or an attorney's letter may provide somewhat the same effect. Is there anything that the nonlawyer can do that will accomplish a similar result? Of course there is.

Where are your opponent's pressure points? How can pressure best be applied? What force is most likely to result in concessions? Sometimes the technique may be as simple as that used by a storekeeper in Maine who, when collecting a delinquent account, ordinarily calls the customer's parents and asks them to "mention" the matter. This technique might not work in Chicago or New York, but in his community close family ties create strong pressures for prompt settlement.

A more unconventional technique was recently used by a militant Episcopalian minister in my neighborhood. When unable to obtain cooperation from a slum landlord on an adjacent block, this clergyman managed to lock the landlord in one of the more verminous empty apartments of his own brownstone, in a room filled with dirty mattresses that this landlord rented to hard-pressed tenants. According to the minister, a few hours of personal contact with the conditions under which his tenants lived persuaded the landlord that it was time to start negotiating with a joint committee of tenants and members of the parish council, with a view toward improving his properties.

Self-help of this kind may lead to criminal prosecution and is not recommended. The incident serves as an example of an extreme technique, which may be necessary as a catalyst before frank discussion can commence between parties in conflict.

A confrontation must be arranged before bargaining can commence. How to do this will depend on the facts of the case.

For example, you may find yourself on the defensive side of a collection action. Is there any way to ward off a lawsuit? Preliminary skirmishing between parties can sometimes be bottled up through correspondence.

A homeowner receives a demand for payment from a tree-maintenance firm that he has hired to prune the trees around his house. He was not satisfied with the way the job was done. Or he may be short of money. At any rate, he does not wish to pay the bill. He must think of some way to delay payment or to avoid it altogether.

When the letter arrives asking him to make payment promptly, he can either ignore it, or answer it in some way that will attempt to delay final resolution. If he chooses to write, the homeowner should not state his objections in terms that require a prompt reply from his antagonist. He should make it as difficult as possible for him to act.

The defensive letter should be designed to inhibit further action. There are a number of ways to do this. For example, the homeowner might tell his creditor that although he is acknowledging his letter, it is necessary for the work to be inspected carefully or perhaps discussed with an expert in the field. Such a proposal, if plausible, may give the homeowner control over the timing of future steps in the dispute. He might then delay several months without doing anything further. In some cases, a defensive letter of this kind may result in many months of protection from further collection efforts.

Another technique is to resist one claim by a demand based on another claim. For example, the homeowner may assert that the pruning actually damaged one of his trees and that he is asserting a claim against the tree service for a larger amount than his bill. This is often done, I am told, by patients who resist medical fees by charging the physician with malpractice.

One attorney told me of a case where a boy received an emergency heart operation which saved his life. In the process, he received a burn on his hip from some malfunction in the operating theatre. When the boy's parents received a bill of several thousand dollars from the surgeons, they sued the hospital and the doctors for malpractice and obtained a reduction in the surgeon's bill as part of the settlement. Such a technique can often be used with success.

Incidentally, this tactic can be the bane of life for a professional who is seeking to collect his fees without the need to take his clients or patients to court. "Many malpractice claims are simply attempts by deadbeats to avoid their obligation to pay for services they have received," is a doctor's sentiment after describing a frustrating collection experience with one of his patients.

Even before you contact the other party, you should review the tactical options that are available. See whether one of them is clearly preferable. At the same time, you should consider whether it may be possible to eliminate some of your opponent's options. Sometimes it is possible to force the other party to fight on less favorable ground.

For example, the alumni association of an eastern university decided to distribute an attractive necktie, featuring a pattern displaying the university's seal to any alumni who gave more than $25 to the annual fund drive. Before the association placed the order, a sample of the tie was submitted by the manufacturer and was made part of the sales contract. The first partial delivery was in accordance with the sample and was accepted without objection. Several weeks later, another shipment was delivered, but these ties had a background that was slightly off color and the insignia was crudely though recognizably executed. The officials of the alumni association objected to the ties for esthetic and practical reasons. The purpose of distributing the ties would be lost if they were not of first-rate quality.

The sales manager for the tie company did not argue too strenuously. He knew that the several thousand ties making up this delivery had been badly manufactured. He did not object to replacing them with a new shipment, produced in accordance with contract specifications. As he pointed out, he was agreeable to taking back the defective ties because he would be able to sell them elsewhere as a novelty item.

The association realized that if these ties were not destroyed, they might be dumped on the market with the result that thousands of men would be wearing inferior copies of the college tie. They asked the maker to destroy the ties. But his sales manager pointed out that the alumni couldn't have it both ways. Either they wanted the ties or they didn't. Either pay for them or return them. He threatened to sue the association if it didn't return the ties.

But the alumni association had already decided what to do. As soon as they discovered that the manufacturer intended to resell them, they destroyed the ties. By "burning their neckties behind them," the association increased its bargaining pressure on the manufacturer. Until the ties were destroyed, he had two options: He could enforce payment or he could retain the ties and sell them. When the ties were destroyed, one option was eliminated.

By taking unilateral action one of the parties can often change the bargaining equation in his favor.

When you first become involved in a dispute, you should consider whether there are any steps that can be taken to strengthen your position. Often such steps have nothing to do with legal processes but concern the subject matter of the dispute itself. Self-help of this type can be extremely useful.

Where your opponent is likely to contest your version of the facts, the truth can be a formidable weapon. One young couple learned how useful it could be to have truth in their corner even before the bargaining begins. About a year before, they had purchased a small parcel of an estate that had been subdivided. They had built their house there. Since then, after the husband had been promoted by his employer, they wanted to purchase an adjacent lot to acquire more space. They made an offer to the real estate agent, which he accepted. The following day the agent called to tell them the deal was off.

"Why?" the husband asked. "I don't understand."

"It's a long story. I'm going to be in your neighborhood this afternoon. I'll stop by and explain why I can't complete the sale."

The young couple were upset. They did not see how the agent could renege. He had accepted the offer. It was their understanding that both parties were legally bound. The husband had an idea: "When he comes this afternoon, why don't we tape the conversation so that we have an accurate record of what he says. If he admits that he sold us the property, we might be able to use the tape to force him to make good on the sale. I'll put the recorder under the couch and turn it on when he comes to the door."

The wife was agreeable. When the agent arrived, they took him into the living room and sat him on the couch. Underneath, the reels of the tape recorder were quietly turning.

"My wife is very disappointed," the husband said. "I remember our conversation quite well. I asked you how much the property would cost us and you gave me a price of $8,000. You told me you were authorized to sell at that price. I took your word for it, and I agreed to buy the property. We shook hands. How can you say that we don't have a contract?"

"I had been told," the agent replied, "that $8,000 was the price. When you agreed to it, I thought the property was sold. This is very embarrassing. When I called the syndicate, they told me I should have asked for more. Now they have a price of $12,000 on the property."

"But how can they do that? When we agreed with you on the other price, we had a deal."

"Ordinarily you would have. Frankly, this syndicate is not operated by gentlemen. Once I told them of your interest, they thought that they could squeeze a higher price out of you."

"How can you lend yourself to that kind of business?"

"Ordinarily I wouldn't. I don't think I'll take on another project with this outfit. But they kind of have you folks over a barrel. We have nothing in writing. Contracts to sell real estate must be in writing. I admit that we had a gentlemen's understanding; under the law that isn't enough. I'm afraid you will have to increase your offer by $4,000."

"Who owns the syndicate?" the husband asked.

"Three men, one of them lives in the large house at the top of the hill. Another is his lawyer. And the third, who put up most of the money, is the president of an insurance company. He lives in New York. But the partner who lives here is the one who makes most of the decisions."

"Does he know that we agreed to buy the property at the price you gave us?"

"Yes, he does. After I talked with him, I called you."

"Would you mind if I talked with him directly?"

"I guess not. I don't know if he would see you, but he might. After all, he lives here, and you're one of his neighbors."

When the agent left, the husband put the tape away, to be used only if necessary. The syndicate owner was a candidate for election to the local country club. The husband happened to be on the membership committee. He mentioned this fact to the syndicate owner when he arranged to meet him. That set the stage.

At first, the visit went pleasantly. Finally, they got around to talking about the younger man's desire to buy the lot next to his house.

"I was shocked by your agent," he said. "We made a perfectly firm bargain. He told me your price and I agreed to it. Then on the very next day, he told me that I would have to pay $4,000 more. He implied that your syndicate intended to welsh on the deal. But, having met you, I can hardly believe that you would be a party to such a practice."

"Did you really make an agreement with our agent? He led me to believe that your conversation had been entirely tentative. The property in this area has continuously increased in value. When we heard that you were interested, we decided to review the asking price. Perhaps that is why the agent told you that you would have to make a higher offer. I can't believe that a definite agreement was reached."

"Perhaps he isn't telling you the whole story. I can assure you that a definite understanding was reached between us. He named the price and I accepted it. We shook hands on the deal. No firmer oral commitment could possibly have been made. I admit that we didn't sign a formal contract—I didn't think I had to. He seemed reliable to me. And I know from your country club application that you are a responsible person. I'm puzzled by the whole situation."

"I'll have to talk to our agent," said the executive. "I'm certain he led me to believe that a final agreement had not been reached."

When the husband returned home, he called the agent. He told him that he had a complete tape recording of their last conversation. He also told him of his conversation with the syndicate owner. "I would suggest that you confirm that you made a binding commitment to sell the property."

Title on the parcel passed to the young couple within the month.

Choosing the Chief Negotiator and His Adversary

Early in the planning, you should decide who will do the negotiating. Sometimes this simply means that you handle it yourself. In a more complicated case, you may want someone to represent you. He should be carefully selected.

Many factors go into this choice. The negotiator must be knowledgeable and experienced, but he must also be someone who understands how bargaining is carried on, and can stand up to the wear and tear of negotiations. This is no job for a weakling or for anyone who is afraid to engage in brinksmanship.

Even when the dispute involves only one person's interests, it is sometimes better for another person to do the talking. For example, a husband may represent his wife. A parent may represent a child. This decision should be made objectively. Not everyone is intellectually or emotionally equipped to carry on important negotiations. If you know that you are not good at this kind of thing, do not try to do it yourself.

The negotiator should have responsibility for identifying the nature of the dispute and for determining the tactical approach. He should have the right to decide whether to call upon necessary experts, such as attorneys.

Does the negotiator have any choice as to his adversary? Must he deal with an attorney, or can he go directly to the other party? Sometimes it is possible to elect the individual with whom he will deal, selecting a weaker, more sympathetic person. An understanding of the available targets is essential. Against corporations this is particularly important. A negotiation should never be launched against an executive lacking the power to make concessions for his company, or the temperament to permit a fair settlement. Often, as much time should be spent finding out about the other party as is spent investigating the case itself.

At the very outset, an investigation should be made of all the facts involved in the controversy. It may provide the key to an informal settlement. For example, the operator of a small airport wanted to increase the revenue from three rent-a-car booths operating in the terminal. First, he analyzed each of the three agencies. He decided that the number one agency could not afford to lose the location, whatever the price. The number two agency would have to follow the leader. Only the number three agency might pull out if the rent was too high.

He negotiated first with the second agency because he also knew that the regional representative with whom he would have to deal was weak and would agree to anything. His hunch was right.

The number two agency promptly agreed to the rental increase, without even bothering to discuss the increase with number one and number three. Number three felt if it was satisfactory to number two, it couldn't be too far out of line. And number one had to come in at the same rental. (This divide-and-rule procedure is often followed in negotiating with tenants.)

The demands for increased rent were backed up by the threat that if any of the agencies did not agree to the increase it would have to find space outside the terminal. The personal weakness of number two, and the emulative nature among rent-a-car agencies generally, contributed to a successful "finesse" by the landlord.

The Use of a Bargaining Agent

Sometimes you can use a bargaining agent. One negotiating goal is to convince the other side that when you have made an offer you are unwilling to make further concessions. This posture may be difficult to maintain when you are handling the negotiations personally. An agent is often used to control the bargaining dialogue.

For example, a lawyer may say to the other party, "I have given you every concession I am authorized to make. I can go no further. My client is not available. And when he becomes available, it will be too late." The lawyer is being used as a shield.

If such a statement is taken at face value by the other party, he may abandon his efforts to obtain further concessions, being convinced that he has to "take-it-or-leave-it." Of course, the lawyer must persuade the other party of his inability to communicate with his client and of the existence of a deadline. Whether or not the inability to communicate and the deadline exist are irrelevant, so long as the other party believes in them.

One man was pressured into buying a Canadian schooner by this technique. The schooner was on the market at an outrageous price. An American doctor fell in love with the boat, after inspecting it on a Sunday afternoon at City Island, New York, where the boat was moored. He told the owner how much he liked the boat. After a brief inspection, he asked the owner what price he would take. The owner told him that he would prefer to have a broker represent him in the transaction. He gave the doctor the name of a yacht broker to call in the morning.

The following day, the broker quoted the price. The doctor made an offer that was several thousand dollars lower.

"No, I'm not authorized to reduce the price," the broker told him. "The owner went back to Canada this morning and told me that no concessions were to be made. I'm afraid that his asking price will have to be met."

Reluctantly the doctor agreed to pay the asking price. He found that he had been badly stung. The boat was worth far less. If he had bothered to have it surveyed and had negotiated with the owner, a much lower purchase price could have been arranged.

I talked to the owner several years later. "When the American doctor came aboard my boat, he seemed so infatuated that I reckoned he would have to have it, whatever the price. I decided to force him to deal through my broker. I instructed my broker not to bargain, and returned to Canada two days earlier

than I had planned. I took a chance. But my gamble was successful. I was delighted to rid myself of the old tub, and at a
satisfactory price."

Not all "horse traders" come from Kentucky.

Making an adversary believe that there can be no further
concessions is a well-known bargaining technique. When representing a corporation, an executive may say that the board of
directors will not permit further compromise. A common example of this technique is the claims adjuster for an insurance
company who tells a claimant that it will be impossible, based
on the facts of the case, for him to obtain authority to increase
his offer. If the claims adjuster can be persuasive on this point,
a claimant is likely to accept the statement at face value.

As one claims manager explained, "Candidly, our function
is to persuade claimants to accept somewhat less than our reserve [the insurance company's evaluation of the case]. We are
purchasing agents. We fix the price list. Usually we settle at
that price. Sometimes a lawyer can push us into a higher
bracket. But not often. Unless we are able to convince the
claimant to accept our price, the case must remain on the court
calendar."

Attempts to convince opponents that an ultimatum has
been made appear in many different bargaining contexts. In
case after case, one or both parties attempt to persuade the
other that no further compromise is possible.

Although lawyers are frequently used as bargaining agents,
others are sometimes better situated and prepared to bargain.

In a complicated situation like the collective bargaining of
large union contracts, operating executives usually represent
the employer. These men are familiar with the problems of
wage and benefit administration. They know the union leadership intimately. They are aware of the practical implications
of changes in the contract language. Although such negotiators
will ask lawyers for advice, they generally handle the bargaining themselves. The same situation often is found in other
conflicts where complicated relationships are involved.

A purchasing agent for a large utility company told me,
"I would no more think of having an attorney negotiate for
'big-ticket' equipment than I would agree to argue a case
myself in the Supreme Court. Unless the negotiator is up-to-
date on the technical and engineering requirements of the

company, he doesn't have enough background to understand the issues. We handle these deals quite independently. I can't remember the last time I talked to one of the company's lawyers."

The Diplomacy of Bargaining

Be sure that the preliminary discussions are handled in a way that strengthens, or at least does not weaken, your position. Bargain from strength. Convince your opponent that you are well prepared, and that you will be firm.

Negotiators should observe customary amenities at the initial face-to-face meeting. Introductions and preliminary conversation often are a useful prelude to serious bargaining. This period should not be thought of as irrelevant to the primary effort, nor should it be approached in an offhand manner.

During the preliminary discussion an attempt should be made to learn as much as possible about the opponent and his point of view. It is sometimes also possible to establish one's own standing and credibility. The emotional tone is often set early in the discussions. As we will see later, it is sometimes helpful to acquire the reputation of being slightly overdemanding.

Practical details must often be worked out, such as planning the agenda for subsequent sessions or determining who should take part in the negotiations themselves. In handling these matters, the experienced negotiator will try to show that he understands his job, that he is aware of the importance of the preliminary details and of the selection of participants. He will be careful not to exhibit a personal anxiety over the future course of the proceedings.

It is seldom sound practice to hurry the discussions. Deliberate conversation is often taken as a sign of confidence. Men who devote their lives to negotiating contested claims are seldom hurried in their approach to the issues. Sometimes they will carry on a seemingly idle conversation until the other party almost screams with impatience, or bluntly plunges into a discussion of the primary topic. Beware. Impatience will be taken as a sign of weakness. The opponent's estimate of what he will have to pay or concede may be reduced as a result. Therefore, the one assigned to negotiate a dispute should be patient, not press the other side, continue an even flow of non-committal remarks, listen and observe, and try to learn as much as possible about the opponent with whom he will be dealing.

An art collector once described a negotiation with a dealer on Madison Avenue, an old hand. The collector went to the dealer's office for the express purpose of making a bid on a valuable china figure. The dealer knew this, but carefully refrained from mentioning it. The collector, suspecting that the dealer was trying to ascertain how much he wanted the piece, talked about other matters. For two and a half hours they discussed everything under the sun, except the purpose of the visit. At the end of that time the collector broke off the conversation.

One week later, the art dealer invited him back. Again the two men sat talking, generally. Finally the art dealer lost his patience and referred directly to the china figure that the collector had come to buy, and the transaction was quickly accomplished. The collector brags that he obtained the piece for less than he was prepared to pay, that he had beaten the dealer at the "patience game."

The personal style of negotiators will vary greatly. A style that best fits the negotiator's personality will probably prove most effective. Some successful bargainers indulge in table thumping and dramatic emotional outbursts. Others avoid histrionics and depend upon a firm but relaxed demeanor. As long as the negotiator can maintain credibility, it matters very little which style he chooses. The table thumper must convince the other party that he is sincerely angry. The stubborn bargainer must conceal any desire to retreat from his position. The negotiator who depends upon a logical presentation must be able to sustain the burden of his logic. And even the rash gambler, who depends upon his ability to convince the other party that he will take irrational and hazardous steps unless a concession is obtained, must be able to play his difficult role to a successful conclusion. The rest is style.

Whatever the approach, if you are the negotiator, it is wise to convince your opponent that you have a full understanding of the circumstances surrounding the dispute. The technical background of the particular controversy should be fully understood and your presentation should incorporate some opportunity for you to show your expertise. The other party will generally be eager to take advantage of any apparent innocence on your part, marking you as a pigeon.

This latter tendency offers an opportunity to play a simulated role. The activator of the "con game" pretends to be an innocent boob, apparently laying himself open for the real "victim" to score a riskless profit. The victim must believe that in taking advantage of an apparently simple person, he can make a safe and secure profit.

Sometime variants of this transaction can be utilized in negotiations. The seller of a house may ostentatiously be oblivious to some valuable feature that the purchaser is bound to notice, hoping that the "poor seller" does not appreciate the full value. Sometime the greed of such a purchaser will make it possible for the seller to avoid disclosing less obvious drawbacks of his property. The impetuous buyer, in his rush to obtain what he thinks is a bargain, may fail to investigate the property.

Designing Your Opener

Success in handling disputes is not a matter of luck or inspiration. After a preliminary investigation of the facts, all relevant information should be drawn together by the negotiator before the discussions begin.

A cartoon shows two prisoners shackled securely to a dungeon wall. One of them says to the other "The first thing! We got to have a plan."

Anyone who intends to initiate negotiations should have a plan of action. Whether the controversy arises in negotiating an award for damages or in settling a family dispute or in resolving a large corporate matter, it is foolish to drift into a negotiation without a plan. Adequate research must first be done as to the nature of the dispute, the motivations and personality of the opponent, and the available steps by which a successful resolution can be obtained. No matter how ominous the power of the other party may be, the negotiator will do better for himself if he follows a well-designed bargaining plan, as opposed to simply defending himself against the other party. Negative negotiation is almost always doomed to failure.

And yet, how frequently we see parties come to an adversary confrontation without a fixed objective. One day, at a negotiating session having to do with changing the terms of a government research grant, I even heard a lawyer lean toward his client shortly after the meeting commenced and whisper, "Why are we here? And what do we want?"

When you enter into negotiations, you should design your original proposals carefully, considering your probable need to make further concessions. Be careful not to make concessions before you have to. Do not give the impression of being so "reasonable" that your opponent will assume that you will be an easy mark.

Initial proposals should exceed what you ultimately hope to achieve. Excessive proposals often are made for the purpose of obtaining concessions. But they should be believable enough for the other side to take seriously.

Sometimes, for purposes of bargaining, you can include a demand that is objectionable to the other side with the aim of gaining concessions quite different from your demand. This is a technique often used by experienced negotiators.

For example, a rather hard-nosed negotiator, when dickering for the purchase of a famous ocean-racing yawl, stubbornly demanded as part of his offer to purchase the boat the right to retain the original name. The seller wanted the name for his new boat, which he confidently expected would also do well on the ocean-racing circuit, bringing further glory to himself as a skipper. This wrangle over the name of a boat became extremely important in the negotiations.

A few months after the deal was closed, the purchaser confided that his concession on the matter of the name had been parlayed into a substantial reduction on the asking price. He had only pretended to like the original name.

This anecdote indicates that different items on the negotiating agenda will have different values to each participant. In this case, the buyer valued the name at zero. But the seller valued it at several thousand dollars. The seller regarded the name as a critical issue, although he was eager to sell. Such issues have a way of becoming particularly expensive.

Arguments used to justify preliminary demands should also be aimed at changing your opponent's point of view. Logical statements as to why such a demand should be acceptable, statements substantiating your position, sales talk in general, threats or implications of disastrous effects should the negotiations break down, all of these techniques can be used to veil your own position. For example, even if you realize that you would be willing to concede on any terms, the worst thing you can do is to let your opponent suspect it. When he knows that you will accept less, he will automatically offer less.

This is elementary. But it is surprising how often a negotiator can be seen exhibiting a craven bargaining position to his opponent.

By too heartily espousing the rule of reason, you may be reducing your ability to take a hard-nosed, unreasonable position at a later stage in the negotiations. Do not convince your opponent that you are a wholly reasonable gentleman. It will cost you.

One young lawyer learned this lesson the hard way many years ago when he was asked by a client to negotiate a separation agreement from her husband, a philandering automobile dealer. The husband was represented by his business attorney, a senior member of a large corporate law firm. At the first settlement conference, the young lawyer was overawed by the austere opponent who faced him across the table.

"I am sure that you do not wish to be unreasonable," the older lawyer said. "My client is perfectly willing to make a fair and adequate settlement. Since I recognize that you are a gentleman, it should be quite easy for the two of us to work out the details."

Like a fool, the younger man fell in with this prattle about fair play and failed to adopt the hostile, unreasonable stance that is most productive in these affairs. He did not sue the husband for divorce. He did not threaten or bully, as most marital practitioners habitually do. No indeed, he fell into the trap of negotiating like a gentleman.

From hindsight, that lawyer believes that his client suffered. He was so sweetly reasonable to the opposing counsel that, after one unsuccessful conference, his client turned to him and said, "What's wrong with you? You sound as if you are afraid to argue. I have a right to what I'm asking. It was his fault, wasn't it? Get in there and fight for my rights."

In negotiations, the meek do not inherit the earth. To win, you may have to threaten the worst, convince your opponent of the high price of battle, and militantly attempt to get your way. To win such battles, it is necessary to fight.

Exploiting the Decent-Man Rule

An initial appraisal should be made of the psychology of your adversary. Will he react to your demands by caving in, or will he mount a bitter struggle? Do not automatically assume that he will put up a fight. Sometimes an adversary will be hanging on his phone, hoping that his opponent will call to discuss a conciliation.

One morning, a dentist came to my office to discuss the threat of a lawsuit by a former patient. He was a nervous little man who absent-mindedly drew pictures of tiny sailboats on my blotter as he talked—an entire regatta gradually appeared on my desk as he described the incident.

In a moment of inattention—he was probably daydreaming about sailing on the Bermuda Race—he had permitted his drill to slip while excavating a girl's molar. The drill slashed across the corner of her mouth, severely gashing her lip.

According to the dentist, the lacerated patient was demanding that he reimburse her for all medical and dental expenses, and for pain and suffering. A surgeon had patched up her lip, and another dentist had completed the dental work. She claimed to have paid a total of $260 in medical and dental expenses. And her lawyer was asking him for an additional $4,000 in damages.

My visitor wondered whether he should retain a lawyer to defend his interests.

He had a number of good reasons for wanting to settle the claim. An out-of-court agreement would help preserve his reputation as a careful dentist. He did not relish having his carelessness exposed in court, or, in fact, before an arbitration panel of dentists. I gathered that patients were seldom injured in this way. It would have been a modest *cause célèbre*. He also realized that the case would take him away from his office for at least a day, and was concerned about the nervous strain of testifying at a hearing. He would much prefer to have the unpleasantness behind him.

On the other hand, he believed that the patient was being unreasonable. She was asking an excessive amount for what he believed to be a minor injury. He had almost convinced himself that he ought to fight rather than settle. He had even made an appointment with an attorney, but wanted my advice on the possibility of arbitrating the claim.

I doubted that the girl would be agreeable to any arbitration before his dental association. I suggested that he might attempt a direct settlement. I asked him whether he thought the girl was a tractable person. She had been his patient for six years. He assured me that prior to this incident they had been on excellent terms. He did not think she was vindictive. He suspected that someone had persuaded her to sue him.

I reminded the dentist of another consideration—his insurance. It would be advisable to discuss the accident with his broker since he might have a duty to notify his malpractice carrier. Many personal injury claims involve insurance questions. In this area the layman often needs professional advice, either from an attorney or an insurance expert, and he should be particularly careful to avoid taking any action that might prejudice his liability coverage or his right to recover against the other party's insurance carrier.

The dentist explained to me that he was inclined not to involve his insurance agent because he believed that the potential damages were small. By recording a claim against his malpractice insurance policy, he felt that he ran a risk of increased premiums in the future.

We continued to discuss the various remedies available. Finally, the dentist convinced himself that he ought to try to settle the dispute himself. I let him use my telephone and he was able to reach the girl at home. First, he apologized profusely. Then he explained to the girl that he would not bill her for any of his work. He would be glad to pay the dentist who finished the work, as well as the surgeon. He also offered to pay her something extra for her pain. And they discussed what would be fair.

After a long but friendly talk, the dentist agreed to pay all her medical bills, and an additional $200 for a complete settlement of her claim. The patient, who had probably been reluctant to sue anyway, seemed relieved to dispose of an unpleasant matter.

It was a perfectly reasonable settlement. Neither party had much to gain from a lawsuit, and neither was the "litigating" type. The dentist, by settling the dispute, was repurchasing a fragment of his reputation as well as avoiding a lawsuit. He was buying many hours of working time which would otherwise have been wasted in preparing for the case and attending the hearing. He was also eliminating an impending source of anxiety. What price nerves?

A simple case like this would probably be settled by most "worried" dentists and "good-natured" patients, and this dentist guessed right when he decided to deal directly with the girl on the assumption that she would be "decent."

The average person would like to work out his own disputes in the same way, but hesitates to do so because he is afraid that he may make a mistake and get into even more trouble. Unfortunately many disputes are not so simple. And sometimes the opponent is not a "decent guy."

Sometimes at first an opponent seems conciliatory. But see how quickly he becomes adamant when you press your demands.

One debtor kept promising to pay from month to month. assuring his creditors that it was simply a matter of withdrawing some cash from his business. He gave one excuse after another why such a withdrawal could not be made. He was extremely polite. In fact, he convinced some of the group to stop dunning him for several months. But finally, he filed for personal bankruptcy.

Then his demeanor changed. No longer was he the solicitous, sympathetic debtor. "Forget it! You had your chance to collect. But I held you off. Now I don't have to lick your boots. Get your money in the bankruptcy court if you can, but for God's sake, stop bothering me."

His obsequious manner had bought time. He had known that he would never have to pay his debts.

How to Use Free Advice

As disputes become more involved, there may be a greater need for parties to bring in outside experts. I have mentioned the value of lawyers in dealing with liability claims. And if an insurance broker is involved, you should feel free to ask him for information as well.

In other kinds of controversies, it is sometimes possible to obtain free advice from a firm that provides a competitive service connected with the matter in dispute. For example, a building contractor will often give an estimate on the expense of repairing defective work. An automobile repair shop will often survey a defective engine job. A realtor will give an estimate on the value of real property.

There are other sources for informed and objective advice. The local Better Business Bureau will investigate defective merchandise. A Chamber of Commerce or bank may advise on the reputation of a local business. Sometimes government agencies might be willing to investigate the other party's activities.

Free advice is not always the best bargain. In one situation an architect was asked to inspect a summer cottage as a favor to the son of a business acquaintance. The architect visited the cottage during a blizzard, and after only a brief inspection pronounced the cottage sound. The young man purchased the cottage on the basis of the opinion. As it turned out, half the beams in the roof were rotten. The architect had accepted $25 for transportation, and because of this the son was able to sue him for malpractice, and recover damages of several thousand dollars.

A free survey is often a slapdash job and is no guarantee of quality. Therefore, where significant interests are involved, it may be wise to pay a fee for expert advice.

A dealer who buys paintings for several midwestern museums discovered a painting in a Madison Avenue gallery that appeared to be substantially underpriced. At the time, he was studying art history at a university night school. He prevailed upon his teacher to inspect the painting. The teacher was enthusiastic, assuring him that the painting was what it purported to be, a valuable original. My friend entered into preliminary discussion with the gallery but, before closing the deal, decided to have the picture appraised by an independent expert, as an extra precaution. At first, the owner of the gallery objected. Whether he suspected the outcome was never clear. At any rate, the appraiser was able to show that the painting was a forgery, a very well-painted one, worth far less than the gallery was asking.

When a significant sum may turn on the accuracy of the advice, it makes sense to go to a qualified professional for an opinion, and to pay for it. This is particularly true when a failure to settle the matter may force both parties into an expensive lawsuit. An expert opinion may narrow the issues and provide a solution, particularly where objective standards are applicable.

This is frequently done in connection with wage disputes. In one social agency the entire staff had threatened to resign unless salaries were increased in line with similar agencies. The Board of Directors asked a management consultant to review the salary scale. The consultant filed a report two weeks later, comparing the agency's salaries with those of twelve similar agencies. His recommendations were accepted by the board, and increases were installed throughout the agency.

As the president of the agency later told me, "If we had done this study ourselves, it would have taken months. Anyway, I don't know where we could have gotten all the facts this consultant was able to obtain. It may seem unusual for a Board of Directors to agree in advance to accept the recommendations of a consultant. But we felt that in this case our agency had gotten so far out of step, that it was only fair to catch up. It worked so well that we are considering doing the same thing next year."

The same technique can be used by individuals where the dispute turns on a question of fact or evaluation.

A widow decided to distribute property to her two sons. She owned a summer house and a substantial portfolio of securities. One Christmas she announced that she intended to give the summer house to her older son and about $40,000 in securities to her younger son. The younger son was outraged, claiming that he was being given substantially less than his brother. The older boy denied this, pointing out that nobody knew how much the house was worth. Neither son was satisfied. Their mother was upset since she had intended to treat them equally. She discussed the problem with her financial adviser.

"Why don't you get an appraisal on the present value of your summer house?" he suggested. "That way, you could give the other son exactly the same amount in stocks, and neither would have any complaint."

That afternoon she called her sons and asked them whether the arrangement would be satisfactory. They agreed. The house was appraised at $36,000. When the mother transferred title to her older son, she also transferred $36,000 worth of securities

to her younger son. As it turned out, the younger son purchased a half interest in the house from his brother for $18,000.

The Need for Accurate Information

Be sure that you thoroughly understand the situation before you embark upon negotiations, and be particularly sure
that you understand your adversary's point of view. Frequently,
you might discover that he sees things quite differently.
In some cases, the controversy is caused by a mutual misunderstanding. (It may later turn out that only you were con-
fused.) Many disputes are caused by lack of knowledge. The
other party may not even know about the misunderstanding
until he is already engaged in an unnecessary and embarrassing disagreement.

A young couple had been living with the husband's parents, but were looking for their own home. They came upon a
set of plans in a magazine for exactly the small house that they
wanted. But it cost too much. For another year they saved
their money. Finally they had accumulated as much as the
magazine said they would need.

They called upon a builder, a small contractor in the
suburban community where they wanted to locate. He looked
over the plans and said that he could build their house within
their budget. They shook hands.

The builder showed them where to find land, and arranged
for them to buy it. Then he started building their "dream
house." Each weekend the young couple would visit the site.
Each time they saw the contractor, they would instruct him to
make minor changes. Sometimes he warned them that these
changes would increase the total cost. But usually he simply
agreed to make the change. Finally the house was completed.

The contractor submitted his final bill. His customers were
shocked. The bill was $5,000 over the amount they had agreed
upon. When they protested to the contractor, he said that the
additional charges covered changes and extras. They must have
understood that it would cost more when they requested a
change in the plans. As he explained, "You wanted changes
made, and changes cost money."

The young couple were not convinced. "Why didn't you

tell us how much it would cost if we ordered changes?" They refused to pay the final bill.

The contractor knew he was right. He had done the work, and he had confirmed each change order by letter. But he was puzzled whether to sue the young couple. They had not understood how expensive their changes would be. If he took the case to court, the jury might feel that he had imposed upon his customers. And even if he won, there would be additional legal costs, delays, and lawyers' fees. Perhaps he was somewhat at fault in not warning them of the increasing costs.

Beyond this, he knew that the couple's neighbors would be told about their problem, and would be sympathetic. He wanted to continue building homes in this community. He could not afford disgruntled customers.

"What should I do?" he asked his attorney.

"Is there any chance of negotiating a settlement?"

"No," the contractor replied. He had tried that, but now the young couple refused to speak to him.

The attorney was able to talk with them. He suggested that the dispute ought to be settled. He told them how expensive it would be to defend their case in court. The lawsuit would delay their occupancy. Finally, he convinced them to submit the dispute to an arbitrator, and suggested a retired lawyer who had lived in the community for over fifty years. Both parties agreed not to be represented by lawyers at the hearing. Only on that basis would the young couple agree to arbitrate. (This is not always recommended. Arbitration can be a dangerous adversary proceeding. A lawyer is often very much needed.)

The arbitrator held a meeting at the new house. He listened patiently while the couple explained that they had not known how much their minor changes would cost. The contractor said little. But he did show the arbitrator a letter confirming the basic cost of the house. And he showed copies of letters confirming each change. Then he pointed out each change to the arbitrator, and showed how much that change had cost him.

Finally, the arbitrator announced his award. He explained to the young couple that ignorance of the law was no excuse. They had asked the contractor to make changes. The changes had cost extra.

On the other hand, the contractor should have warned the young couple of the extra charges being caused by their frequent suggestions. "After all," the arbitrator told the contractor, "You are an experienced businessman. Obviously, they are not."

The arbitrator did not think it was fair for the contractor to include any profit in the cost of making the changes. He awarded the contractor his exact costs. The young couple were not able immediately to pay the entire amount owed, but they paid most of it. The balance was paid in monthly installments during the following year.

After the hearing, the contractor apologized to his customers. They forgave him, and eventually recommended him to several of their friends who were moving into the area.

The lawyer who served as arbitrator in this case was pleased by the result. As he explained it to me, he felt that his decision had resolved the problem to everyone's satisfaction. His compromise had seemed to please both parties, probably because both were partially responsible for the dispute.

"After a client tells me about his claim," one trial lawyer told me, "I always try to put myself in the other fellow's position. How do the facts look to him? Why is he refusing to pay? Why would a reasonable person be contesting my client's claim? This mental exercise makes it possible for me to ask the correct questions, to investigate in the right places, and to appraise the potential of my case."

But do not assume that your opponent will act in a logical and reasonable way. You are not dealing with a computer. The human factor must be appraised.

Sometimes an argument may seem to occur for perfectly logical reasons, but unsuspected causes may underlie the conflict and block the parties from compromising their differences.

In one situation, the lease in a new office building required the landlord to provide adequate air conditioning. After the tenant company took possession, it was discovered that some of the interior rooms were uncomfortably hot. Particularly where equipment such as copying machines generated additional heat, the air-conditioning system did not seem adequate. The president of the tenant corporation took up the dispute as a crusade against the landlord, harassing him with frequent telephone calls.

The building superintendent adjusted the air-conditioning system over and over again. Finally the president requested his lawyer to notify the landlord that if the air conditioning was not substantially improved, it would be necessary for the company to sue.

Since none of the other tenants in the building had complained about the air conditioning, the owner of the building wondered about this particular tenant. He asked the president of the company to have lunch with him. As he expected, he had to submit to a tirade about the services in the building, with particular emphasis upon the air conditioning. The owner quickly promised to try to improve the air conditioning, but his main objective was to learn more about the president himself. Was he the real problem?

He discovered that the president of the tenant company was a hypochondriac who suffered from colds throughout the entire year, and that he had installed a temperature control system in his own home that maintained the temperature within a range of five degrees, winter and summer. Obviously, the problem in the office building was related to the man's personality. What to do?

When he returned to his office, the owner of the building called in the building manager. "Stop worrying about the air conditioning in the working areas," he said. "But make sure that the air conditioning in the president's office is correctly set. And spend some time with the president's secretary. See that she knows how to operate the dial so that the temperature is always the same in his office. Tell her that we are trying to do everything possible to make her boss more comfortable. Tell her to let you know of the first sign of a problem with the temperature in his office. And give her something nice to keep from reminding him of the air-conditioning problem."

The owner of the building then called up the tenant's lawyer. He told him that he was taking steps to improve the air conditioning. He asked for time so that this could be accomplished. He thought he could guarantee that no complaints would be made in the future. The lawyer was agreeable.

The president lost interest in the problem as soon as the

temperature in his office was corrected. Because of his secretary's cooperation, minor complaints from the office working areas were no longer brought to his attention. Thus, the owner of the office building was able to resolve a threat that might have grown into prolonged and expensive litigation.

In other situations the impediment to settlement may be faulty communications between the parties. Any method by which transmittal of information can be facilitated will usually increase the likelihood of mutual agreement.

Not always. As a professor at Columbia Law School pointed out to me recently, "Some facts actually drive the parties apart." For example, during negotiations between an individual and an insurance company in connection with an automobile accident, evidence that tends to show that the plaintiff was negligent or that the defendant was not negligent may help the insurance company win. Such evidence might tend to make settlement *less* likely.

But ordinarily the more facts the parties share, the narrower will be their range of disagreement.

The Compadre and the Search for Power

In South America disputes are often resolved by the intercession of a powerful friend of the disputant, his *compadre*. The same technique is equally effective in other societies.

Most people have access to leading citizens in their communities. These men can lend a hand in a particular dispute, and are often willing to do so. For example, a member of Rotary can find another member who can exert power over an organization that is giving him trouble. Sometimes one's employer is willing to play this role. Or an official in one's religious organization. Most Americans have such contacts. But they sometimes forget to use them.

Somewhat the same technique can be used where the dispute is with another individual. Perhaps a member of your opponent's family, his employer, a religious leader, or an influential friend can assist you. Try to find someone who can persuade the other party to do what you want him to do. In modern urban society, most people are subject to pressure points of various kinds that can be identified from a cursory investigation of their personal lives, businesses, or families.

Consider your own situation. How many people are there in your life who could bring compelling pressure to bear upon you? Even a mild suggestion from your employer, your best customer, or your banker might persuade you to abandon an arbitrary position in a controversy. Whenever you engage in a fight, you should take an inventory of the available pressure points you can use, and that can be used against you. For this kind of fighting, you do not need the courts and you can hardly use a lawyer. In fact, in this area lurk the dirtiest of all techniques: blackmail, extortion, and threats. But where your claim is fair and equitable, there is nothing wrong in bringing the matter to the attention of appropriate persons. For example, the manager of a laundry in a small midwestern town agreed not to operate a competing laundry for a period of twenty years. But finding that his salary did not provide an adequate income, he resigned and purchased a "noncompeting" business, a linen rental service for hotels and restaurants in the area.

The owners of the laundry threatened to sue him. They claimed that the linen rental business was in direct competition with the laundry business. Their former manager could not afford to go to court. Instead he tried to work out a settlement. He pointed out that none of the cleaning that he would be doing had ever been done by the laundry. Nor did he intend to compete with the laundry. But the owners of the laundry were not satisfied and filed a summons and complaint in the local court.

Desperately seeking some way to resolve the matter without litigation, this man discussed the problem with the president of a local union that represented the workers in both facilities. He had done favors for this union official while he was managing the laundry, and now felt that he needed a favor in return. Furthermore, he explained that if he were put out of business, union members would lose their jobs. He made his proposal: "Perhaps someone could talk to the owners of the laundry to make litigation unnecessary."

The president of the union was glad to help. He talked with the two brothers who owned the laundry. "This is off the record," he said. "But my union has an interest in this. We don't want either of your companies to suffer. Why don't you tell me what you are really afraid of? Perhaps I can help."

The brothers were willing to talk. They were mainly concerned with the possibility that their former manager, for whom they had great respect, would expand his linen service into the general laundry field. They knew that he would be a hard competitor. If they could be assured that the linen service would not compete with them, they would withdraw their lawsuit. The union leader went back to the owner of the linen service, obtained his consent and then arranged a meeting with both parties, at which a verbal agreement was reached covering the jurisdiction of the two companies.

The owner of the linen service later told me, "My God, I had almost given up. If this thing had gone into court and had been decided by a judge, I have no idea of how I would have come out. But I do know that I could not have afforded to fight the case! I was lucky that my labor friend was willing to intercede. It would have been a shame to have allowed this problem to wreck my business at the very beginning."

Sometimes, the *compadre* may not be directly connected with your opponent's business. Often a political leader will have an equal amount of influence. A gentleman farmer sold a hunting horse, delivering it in return for a certified check. The purchaser took the horse to a veterinarian. To the purchaser's surprise, the horse was declared unsound. He stopped payment on the check.

When the seller deposited the certified check, the bank refused to honor it. He was outraged and went directly to the local branch manager, who apologized but said that he could do nothing. The seller's cousin happened to be a member of the Banking Committee of the state legislature. He called his cousin and asked for help. The cousin called the president of the bank, asking him to look into the matter. Within an hour, the seller received a telephone call from his branch bank. The manager apologized for his error and agreed to honor the certified check.

Not everyone can call upon a relative or friend who has access to high places, and many are reduced to less powerful weapons. This is particularly true of the poor, in the battle between the consumer and the businessman. The courts have not always been an adequate forum. The legal obligation of the buyer to beware, combined with the seller's opportunity to design the sales contract, tends to create a protective envelope around transactions. And so the purchaser finds little comfort in court. His only hope is to generate some outside pressure to persuade the retail store to relent.

Middle-class people can obtain fair treatment from retailers simply because they represent future buying power and can state an articulate case to the complaint department. But poor people, who often have purchased on credit, and not always from the most reputable outlets, have less likelihood of being successful.

Now, through the Poverty Program, the poor are being offered a *compadre* in the legal services offices. As Theodore Voorhees, president of National Legal Aid, explains "What can legal services to the poor accomplish? In the first place, in an encounter with the law—whether in a police court or as to a levy on household furniture—the slum dweller has a lawyer to plead his cause, and a great onslaught is made on defeatism. Antagonism and suspicion will not disappear overnight, but a lawyer's assistance will break down barriers and show the poor they have rights that are worthy of protection. The power of the victimizer—whether he is a landlord, a constable, or a loan shark—will be lessened, if not broken."

How to Use Professional or Trade Associations

If you recall the case of the dentist, you may have wondered why the patient was willing to settle her claim at such a modest figure. If she had threatened to go to the dental society, an important pressure point in the life of any dentist, doubtless she could have increased her settlement. I wondered about this at the time. In fact I congratulated the dentist on what I took to be his good fortune. That patient could easily have brought more pressure to bear on him. In dealing with professionals, as well as with businessmen, you should remember that their associations probably maintain some form of grievance procedure. If a member engages in unethical practices, this remedy should be considered.

There may be more than one association. For example, my association directory lists a total of eleven national associations in the coal industry alone. In dealing with a businessman in the coal industry, several of these associations might provide a useful lever in negotiations. Sometimes, such associations are independent of each other. Some are strong. Some are powerless. Where you have a dispute with a member, you should find out whether any of these associations is likely to contribute to your bargaining power.

I am suggesting that your opponent may be sensitive to pressure brought upon him by his own industry. Although some associations will automatically defend the actions of a member, the mere process of finding out whether your allegations are true will make it necessary for the association to express an interest in the matter. Most professionals and many business-men are sensitive to this type of inquiry. In order to avoid involving their association in the dispute, they may for the first time begin to negotiate seriously with you. This approach is not always successful, but it may be worth a try.

When you approach a trade or professional association, it is usually best to make your initial contact with one of its leaders. Do not talk initially with a staff functionary if you can help it. Each association has a hierarchy. It is preferable that your case drop down from the apex of the hierarchy rather than struggle upward through the feeble hands of officious functionaries. Contact the president or a member of the board of directors, or some official who is highly respected within the organization. If such a person refers you to a committee chair-man or a staff member, you can be sure that your grievance will receive more attention than if you had gone directly to him.

Many trade associations are controlled by a relatively small clique. Where you find this to be true, it is wise to approach the association through one of the clique. This is one of the basic rules in manipulating influence. Carefully select indi-vidual targets. This is especially effective in small communities. There, members of the power structure can accomplish miracles in helping to resolve controversies.

Some trade associations themselves have an Achilles heel. For example, one would expect the Incinerator Institute of America to be particularly sensitive to charges of air pollution. If your dispute were to involve allegations of pollution against one of its members, the institute might lend its good offices to settling the matter to avoid bad publicity. Perhaps the associa-tion would suggest to its members that the issue be resolved

privately. Trade associations often urge their members to utilize settlement procedures that do not disclose embarrassing
information in court. It can be helpful to involve the other
party's industry in your dispute, particularly where the other
party is clearly in the wrong.

The executive director of a small manufacturers' association put it this way: "Let's face it. My salary is paid by the
dues of the larger and more reputable members of this industry. They want me to pressure the marginal operators to
deal fairly with their customers. When a customer comes to
me with a justifiable complaint about one of our members, my
job is to help him. Representing the industry, we persuade the
manufacturer to make good. If more customers knew they
could get help from me, there would be less litigation in our
industry."

He described a recent case he had handled. The Better
Business Bureau had called him to report a large number of
defective products that were appearing in local discount stores.
He checked into it and found that the manufacturer, one of his
smaller members, after merchandise was returned by an original buyer, had sold it through marginal retail outlets. The
product had a mechanical defect that made it inoperative within
a short time after it was purchased.

He called the manufacturer: "Unless you take back this
merchandise I'm going to report the situation to my executive
committee. Our industry can't afford to have defective products
on the market."

At first the manufacturer protested that he had not known
of the defect when the products were sold to the discount
houses. But my informant knew this was not true. He had
obtained a copy of the original rejection letter, which stated
exactly what had been found wrong with the first shipment.

"You knew this product was a lemon. The industry is
going to see that you take it off the market. Yes or no?"

The answer had to be yes. This is the kind of private self-
regulation that all industries are capable of carrying out.
It may provide a practical alternative to the purchaser who
discovers he has been sold inferior merchandise.

Some trade associations feel so strongly about the advis-
ability of keeping their members' dirty laundry out of court
that they require members to submit disputes to arbitration,

either before an arbitration board of the association itself or before some other impartial tribunal. For example, the New York Stock Exchange requires its members to arbitrate all disputes with each other, on pain of discipline if they resort to the courts. This would seem sensible. Even where one of the parties is an outsider, the association may try to persuade him to dispose of the matter privately. Industries that spend millions of dollars to improve their images would be foolish to permit the shoddy business practices of a single member to be publicized in a court trial.

Utilizing the Government—or Fighting It

Sometimes the government will assist one party to a dispute. The local Consumer Frauds Bureau, the Federal Trade Commission, and various municipal licensing bureaus may be worth contacting. The district attorney and the police often are power outlets to consider.

The aggressive citizen should never forget the power of the Bureau of Internal Revenue, at least as a means of punishing an adversary. But tread delicately here. The threat of disclosure of tax liability should not be lightly made. And in any case, an attempt to chastise an opponent may fail to result in any tangible benefit, only in personal gratification. The present posture of rent control in New York City is an example of a government agency established to help tenants. Traditional litigation between tenants and landlords has been substantially replaced by the use of the governmental third force. The threat of intervention by this agency is frequently enough to resolve disputes in favor of the tenants.

I know one tenant who sends a complaint to the Rent Commissioner every time he wants to talk with his landlord. As he explained it to me, "Why not, what else do I get for my taxes?" He keeps a stack of complaint forms on his bedroom bureau. And he serves as a voluntary "shop steward" for the entire apartment house.

It is not unusual for an opponent in the conflict game to be a branch of government. Then there may be other sources of power. Congressmen are often willing to lend their names to an individual's grievance in a complaint against a federal agency if it seems plausible. And many of these agencies have investigation and review procedures, although here one may need expert advice, because agency complaint procedures are complex and sometimes ineffectual.

Remedies against the government may sometimes involve obscure, shifting, but effective byways that circulate around and through the offices of administrative agencies, lobbyists, and trade associations. Some lawyers and lobbyists achieve a reputation for obtaining gratifying results for clients without ever having to utilize the tedious procedures government regulations would seem to require. These men should not be dismissed as "fixers" or "power brokers."

They carry out the very legitimate function of bringing the citizen or businessman in contact with the appropriate arm of government.

A middle-aged salesman for a uniform company happened to sit beside me on the Washington–New York air shuttle. He told me about the first time he tried to sell uniforms to the Navy: "I carried my case up and down endless halls trying to find someone to talk to for three of the most discouraging days of my life. I never seemed to be making my spiel to the right person. I was about to give up. Then I happened to call a friend of mine in our industry trade association. Right away he put me in touch with the right man. From then on, I have never had any trouble finding out how to do business with the Navy. That was a mighty profitable telephone call."

In another situation, a local recreation program was bogged down by delay in obtaining funds from a Federal agency. The grant had been approved. But the money was not forthcoming. Finally a member of the board, a prominent New York attorney, made a telephone call to the secretary of another agency. They had roomed together in law school and were close personal friends. By the end of that same business day, the bureaucratic process had been expedited. The check was on its way.

For purposes good or bad, personal relationships with relevant public officials should not be overlooked. The government is run by people. They can move slowly or swiftly. They can help or hinder. Pressure can be brought to bear.

Businessmen who negotiate for government contracts are particularly familiar with the tactical moves that obtain preferences over competitors. This is a never-ending process. Government officials are entertained by contractors. Intermediaries are retained and utilized. Political pressures are brought to bear. Publicity is used aggressively to arouse public opinion at appropriate times. Secret but immensely important private interests jockey to obtain profits from government contracts.

An executive with a huge defense contractor put it this way. "With over 60 percent of the government budget going into defense expenditures, this is where the action is. We will pay almost anything to the man who can get what we want from the government. And we don't much care how he does it. We think we are producing good products. And we know how to present them. Beyond that, we need to know everybody on the government side who might influence the final decision. Our business is too important to leave anything to chance."

An individual who has a dispute with a government agency should try to copy these tactics. Anyone with stationery and a typewriter can saturate the officials of the agency involved—senators, congressmen, and anyone else who can be helpful. Pull every string you can. Personal contacts should be exploited. Within the limits of one's capacity and interest, the game should be played to win.

When you are dealing with a municipal or state government, the opportunities for guerrilla advocacy are probably even more rewarding. Local government is extremely sensitive to pressure by groups of citizens, particularly when those citizens have an apparently valid claim.

The Role of the Mediator

Sometimes an impartial person who can serve as a mediator can be brought into a dispute by the parties. This is an option that should be considered if both parties are serious about reaching a conclusion.

A mediator makes settlements happen. He facilitates voluntary agreement in whatever way he can. He may attend conferences with both parties at the same time. Or he may talk with one at a time. He may simply be a conduit for transmitting information between them. At other times, he may edit the message. He transmits offers, injects new information into the negotiations, encourages parties to continue bargaining, and suggests new agendas for discussion. His is the task of persuading the parties to keep moving toward each other until they reach final agreement.

The talents of the mediator are extremely important.

The mediator cannot require either party to change his position. To that extent, he is impotent. Parties can discontinue his services at any time. In fact, either can reject him.

There are no schools for training mediators. Government agencies that provide mediation services ordinarily train newly employed mediators by letting them work with experienced men. Somewhat informally the new man obtains the benefit of accumulated experience. No formal training seems to be available.

A mediator must be able to understand the issues and to express himself clearly when he transmits information or suggests possible solutions to the parties. He must be able to sell them his ideas, control his emotions, and to inject useful humor into the proceedings when appropriate. To do this, it may help to be "one of the boys."

Above all, he must be a man whose impartiality is acknowledged by both factions. He must also know when not to participate in the bargaining. Sometimes only the parties can hammer out the dimensions of a deal. Another useful characteristic is the ability of a mediator to show inventiveness and originality in the suggestions that he makes. Some of the most outstanding mediators have this characteristic.

Sometimes, the mediator has to use tricks to bring parties together. On the verge of agreement over a million-dollar real estate deal, a frustrated lawyer told the other party to "quit chiseling." Negotiations were broken off in anger, although both sides had much to gain from the contract. A banker who was financing part of the project wanted to reconcile the parties. He adopted a well-known strategy of mediation. He invited both parties to meet him at his office, but in separate rooms. He told each side that the other was there, eager to resume negotiations. He implied that he hesitated to bring them together because he was afraid they would quarrel. By saying this, he insured that each faction would be careful to avoid a fight. Only then, did he bring them together. It worked. Both groups were on their best behavior and the talks moved swiftly to a conclusion.

Every businessman constantly exercises conciliation skills. He may not always be aware that he is "mediating." When the president of a manufacturing company "works out" a disagreement between his marketing director and his production manager over a new product, he is more likely to be mediating than making a decision.

One corporate president is proud of the fact that he spends the major part of his time resolving disputes within his own organization, "always by agreement, never by jamming it down their throats. Unless an executive thinks that it was his decision, he is unlikely to carry it out. I like to compromise, not dictate."

Sometimes mediation is not enough: a fact-finder is required. While a contractor had been preparing a secret bid on a new school building, one of his employees had been seen talking with his competitor's president. The competitor had then bid in the job a few hundred dollars below his own bid, and the contractor concluded that his employee had disclosed the bid. Had he been bribed? The contractor filed charges against his competitor with the Board of Governors of its trade association. When the secretary of the association discussed the case with the competitor, he was assured that the charge was not true. He then suggested that the principals ask a fact finder to investigate. A leading local lawyer was asked to carry out an investigation of the charges.

The fact finder spent three days talking with witnesses for both sides. He discovered that meetings had occurred between the competitor and the employee: they concerned an offer of employment. When the fact finder was sure of the truth, he called the two principals together and gave them a full report. He was satisfied that the accused contractor had not been aware of the amount of the first bid on the school job.

The plaintive contractor thanked him for the facts, went back to his office, apologized to the offending employee for suspecting him—and fired him. "Any man who works for me," he growled, "should have more sense than to meet secretly with my competition."

The trade association executive had suggested a procedure for discovering the facts. But he was careful not to get involved in the controversy. Mediation can be used in the same way.

Success is not always possible. I remember one case involving a decorating business, where the mediator failed because he had once known one of the parties too well!

Two sisters-in-law had established a decorating business in New York City that seemed a fine idea. Sally had talent; Jane had inherited money from an aunt.

As Jane pointed out, "I have the capital. You have the experience and the talent. I will be able to get customers. And you will train me to help with the job." So the two women went into business.

At first it was a success. But gradually Jane became involved in nonbusiness activities. Increasingly, she served on charity benefit committees, with much of her time going to social events. At first Sally did not mind, because some of the people that Jane met became clients of the firm. But Jane lost interest in the business. Because she had supplied the initial capital, she felt that it was only fair for her partner to run the business, and also do the selling. The partners gradually grew apart, Jane doing progressively less, Sally more. When they discussed their business, they quarreled. It became apparent that they were no longer partners.

The bickering between the ladies reached their husbands' ears. The brothers decided that in the interest of keeping peace, the partnership ought to be dissolved. Sally should buy out Jane at half the value of the business. But when they suggested this to their wives, their proposal was rejected.

Jane felt that her share should be more than half, since her money had started the business, and many of the original clients had been hers. Sally felt that she should pay less than half because her personal contribution had been the significant factor in making the business a success. Nor could they agree how much the business was worth.

The brothers decided that the best way to handle the matter was for them to fix a sales price, which they would submit to their wives. This, they did. Neither wife was satisfied. In Jane's case, the disagreement at home almost dwarfed the original dispute.

Soon afterward the brothers met at their lunch club. While they were discussing their predicament, they were joined by a mutual friend who happened to be a business consultant. They told him their domestic problem. "Why not let me handle it?" he volunteered, "I would be glad to try to establish a fair figure for the value of the business. I'll arrange a meeting with your wives. Don't tell me the figure you suggested. Let me take a fresh look at the whole thing." The brothers were delighted, and agreed to permit this good Samaritan to mediate the dispute.

Unfortunately, many years before, their mutual friend had been an admirer of Jane's. This was known to both ladies, but not to their husbands. Although Jane and Sally agreed to meet him at the Colony Club for lunch, neither considered the mediator impartial. Jane was afraid that he might presume upon their prior relationship. Sally feared that he would favor Jane.

The mediator soon sensed that conciliation would not work. The ladies' attitude toward him was icy, although he did not know exactly why. As a last resort, he suggested that the dispute be submitted to an impartial arbitrator. On the back of a menu he scribbled down a description of the dispute, with an agreement that it be arbitrated. Both ladies signed the menu, which he then mailed to the American Arbitration Association. He was so glad to rid himself of the difficult task of mediating between two temperamental women, that he paid the administrative fee himself.

The case came before an arbitrator, a branch bank manager. The partners presented their financial figures for the prior two years, with a register of their clients. Ten days after the hearing, the arbitrator announced his award, establishing a price for the business. Sally, the continuing partner, paid Jane for exclusive rights to the business. Although the price was almost the same as the figure set by their husbands, it was acceptable to the ladies and the award made it possible for the partnership to be sold.

Professional mediators and conciliators are active in only a few fields. Labor relations is one. The Federal Mediation and Conciliation Service maintains a nationwide staff of mediators who devote themselves to working with management and labor, trying to expedite collective bargaining agreements. Family counselors play a somewhat similar role in dealing with disputes between husbands and wives. And in a few other settings, conciliators are paid by government or private agencies to work with parties in resolving their differences. But these are specialized areas of controversy. No generalized mediation profession has yet evolved. However, expert mediators are asked to serve in other contexts. In recent years we have seen a drift of the leading labor management impartials into other areas of controversy. For example, labor arbitrators and mediators with long experience with unions and private employers have helped resolve government employment disputes, civil rights issues, and even disputes between nations.

The president of a local trade association called my office one day and asked for help. His association was seeking a merger with another in the very same industry. He was worried that the discussions would break down unless they were chaired by an experienced mediator. Would we invite the associations to meet and provide a chairman?

Our chairman was accepted by both sides and the meetings began. Almost at once an impasse developed. Then the mediator went to work, asking the association leaders to explain their positions on various isues. They were far apart. After two days of meetings, he persuaded them to accept a compromise formula.

One of the negotiators later told me that agreement would have been impossible without the participation of the impartial chairman. As he put it, "Every time our group was ready to walk out, that guy would come up with some new gimmick to keep us talking. Where did he learn all those tricks? This merger is something that we should have done long ago. But for him, we never would have gone through with it."

"What tricks did he use?" I asked.

"The first thing he did was to spend enough time with each side to gain a full understanding of each position. He let us talk ourselves out. Then he kept asking questions until he knew more about our operations than we did. Before he was through, he had made us analyze exactly what we wanted and what we thought the other side wanted. He did the same thing with them. For the first time, both sides understood what the negotiations were about. Then he began to make suggestions

how various items might be compromised. By now we were
pretty close. To bring us the rest of the way, he would call in
the officers of each association, one by one, or in small groups,
trying to persuade each individual that he had more to gain
from the merger than he had to lose. Finally, he called a joint
meeting and laid out the whole deal. This was about midnight
on Sunday. One guy tried to hold out for some personal advantage he wanted, but the group shouted him down. They
wanted to get home. Before the chairman would let us go, he
wrote down the terms of our agreement and made everyone
sign. It was a beautiful job."

Parties in dispute sometimes resist the intervention of an
impartial person on the basis that no outsider should be privy
to their disagreement. This may be a mistake. A mediator can
often help them reach a resolution. Where the controversy is
important to the public at large, government authorities should
sometimes require that a mediator attend the negotiating sessions.

The individual disputant should decide whether it may be
to his advantage to involve an outsider. Someone not directly
concerned in the dispute may have an interest in seeing that it
is settled. Each controversy should be analyzed to see if such
persons exist.

For example, two small storekeepers who were located in a
shopping center became involved in a bitter dispute over who
should clean the common sidewalk between their stores. Each
tenant was obligated to sweep his half of the sidewalk and to
keep it clear of snow and litter. The stores kept different hours.
One half would often be clean and the other dirty. Sometimes
an employee would sweep litter from one side onto the other.
The storekeepers constantly quarreled about this minor but
irritating dispute.

One of them decided to discuss the matter with the owner
of the shopping center, who called a meeting with the two
shopkeepers. With his help, the matter was soon adjusted by
having one store sweep the entire sidewalk in the morning and
the other clean it in the evening. This system benefited both
parties and solved their problem.

Sometimes an arbitrator will decide that a case before him
ought instead to be mediated. One such case involved a three-
man panel. Two of the arbitrators had been appointed by the

parties themselves. The parties were two large corporations represented at the hearing by attorneys. As the neutral arbitrator listened to the lawyers' opening statements, he realized that the case involved the credibility of two junior executives. Which of these men was lying?

"It is too bad that two outstanding corporations have to waste their valuable time in contesting this insignificant case," one of the party-appointed arbitrators commented.

The chairman took the cue. He spoke to the two attorneys, "Before we begin to take testimony, I wonder if you would be willing to discuss some of the issues with me. As my colleague has suggested, this case ought to be settled. Sometimes a simple misunderstanding can create an issue of truthfulness. Then any decision that an arbitrator makes will have the effect of punishing one side or the other. To avoid this result, I have found that mediation is often helpful. I would suggest that both parties let me meet first with the president of one company, and then with the president of the other. I do not promise anything. And if you are unable to reach a compromise after we have gone through the mediation process, you may wish to disqualify me as an arbitrator. I will take that risk."

One lawyer quickly agreed. In fact, he pointed out, "We've been trying to persuade these people to sit down with us for over five months. They haven't been willing to lay their cards down face up."

The other attorney was hostile, but did not reject the suggestion. "I don't care how much time we waste. I'm prepared to come to New York time after time, until we can thrash out every issue involved. This is not a simple case. If you believe that it might be possible to clarify the issues through mediation, I will not object to my client participating. But I do reserve the right to challenge your impartiality if the mediation process is unsuccessful."

The chairman of the arbitration panel met with the presidents, separately. Their companies had done business together for many years. But not any longer. Their relationship had been destroyed by this disagreement. Each president told the mediator that the other was a liar and a cheat. The mediator patiently listened to their accusations, but also asked questions about the facts of the case. He discovered justice on both sides. After he understood their positions, it was possible for him to begin mediating. By talking first to one and then to the other, he obtained mutual concessions until only $700 separated them from a complete settlement.

At that point, he changed his tactics. He called in the attorneys. "Gentlemen," he said, "as you know, I have spent most of the morning with your clients. I now think that I know how a possible compromise might be reached. I have not yet been able to persuade your clients to settle but they are not far apart. In fact only $700 separates them. I need your help to accomplish the final step. Please see if you can't persuade them to split the difference."

The attorneys met with their clients and were able to obtain agreement on the final concession. From hindsight, both presidents were delighted with the mediation. "We would have been foolish to have persisted in arbitrating this case," one said. "My vice president overstated the facts out of loyalty to me, and it would have come out in the hearing. I didn't want to endanger his reputation just to win this case. I am glad that the arbitrator took the initiative in settling our dispute."

Chapter 4

SETTLING THE MOST
COMMON DISPUTES

Some of the most common disputes likely to be encountered are customarily resolved out of court. Important disagreements between husbands and wives, parents and children, and even business partners are almost always susceptible to amicable settlement, if adversaries will explore the possibilities. Tempers may run high in these areas and the partys' capacities for rational accommodation may suffer, but the overwhelming logic of avoiding litigation usually convinces them that a lawsuit would be senseless.

With such incidents, negotiating techniques can be quite informal. Members of the family can play adversary roles, or serve as mediators. Partners in a warring firm can try to help their contesting fellow partners; sometimes a client can be asked to lend a hand. Generally, where the relationships of the parties are close and personal, someone can be called in to help resolve disagreements.

This chapter will also deal with several other common dispute settlement areas—how to collect on a claim for personal injuries, obtain payment of an overdue account, bargain over payment of a professional fee, and how to manage controversies with home improvement and construction contractors. These are the kind of day-to-day problems that can be handled more effectively with intelligent bargaining techniques and the avoidance of common mistakes.

Often, parties can resolve disagreements without assistance but great care should be taken not to prejudice one's position in case litigation becomes necessary. For the injured person seeking to collect damages from an auto insurance company or someone seeking to collect a debt, it is important to realize that claims can be made personally and that there are recognized techniques for making recovery more likely. Such matters should be handled methodically, in much the same way that professional collection agents or claim adjusters would handle them. The facts should be carefully mustered and presented in a straightforward manner. The credibility of the claimant should be established so that his assertions will be believed. The claimant must convince his adversary that he knows the full value of his claim, is prepared to persevere in collecting the full amount, and is not afraid to go to court if necessary. The other party must believe that he will have to make payment and that it will have to be an adequate amount. If a claimant seems to flag in his effort to collect, it is likely that the debtor will assume that payment need not be made.

Family Dissension

Disputes between relatives are often extremely bitter, scarred by extensive and vicious litigation, highlighted by extreme emotionalism. You should never be drawn into such a dispute without giving thought to the opportunities you may have for resolving it in your favor, or trying to understand what the underlying cause of the controversy may be, or lining up the action opportunities that are available to you.

Why are family arguments so bitter? One psychiatrist believes that the problem is that people see their family bonds in different ways. "Who is obligated to whom?" he asks. "Are the parents bound to make sacrifices for their children? And when does the obligation change, so that the children should begin to support their parents? Nobody agrees on these things, least of all the members of a particular family. No wonder there is constant conflict and anxiety between generations within each family. No wonder we see so many families fly apart under economic stress."

The financial demands of one relative upon another do indeed underline many family squabbles. These disputes can range from the probings of a twelve-year-old for an increased allowance to dramatic litigation between collateral relatives over the inheritance of a millionaire's estate.

A squabble over the refund of private school tuition is a good example of an irrational situation which could have been entirely avoided.

The dispute involved a wealthy couple I will call the Suttons. They lived in Greenwich, Connecticut, and had a daughter named Dorothy. One early spring, the mother enrolled Dorothy for her second year in a private boarding school in New England. Under the contract, half of the yearly tuition had to be paid in advance. The school was family owned and depended on tuition for most of its income.

Soon after Mrs. Sutton signed the contract, the family went to Bermuda for the Easter vacation period. There the Suttons stayed at a beach club and met another couple from Greenwich who also had a teen-age daughter and were a cut above the Suttons in the Greenwich social hierarchy. One morning the two mothers met on the club terrace, sipping daiquiris and discussing their daughters' schools. The other girl went to a more fashionable school in Virginia, which according to her mother, was particularly good for "gifted" children. (Mrs. Sutton had always believed Dorothy to be a "gifted" child.)

That evening Mrs. Sutton had an argument with her husband. She suggested that they ought to transfer Dorothy to the new school in Virginia. He called her a snob. She told him that she was suggesting it only to help him—that if he was ever going to get ahead in business, he could do it only by meeting people like her new friend. Mr. Sutton refused to transfer Dorothy to the new school and they ended by having a violent quarrel.

Back in Greenwich, Mrs. Sutton wrote to the New England school to say that she hand changed her mind about having Dorothy return in the fall. She explained that she wanted to transfer her daughter to another school, and asked for a refund of her deposit. She received no answer.

In August, Mr. Sutton received a letter informing him that his obligation for the first half of the annual tuition was fixed by contract, and that the school was refusing to refund his payment. Mr. Sutton was furious and asked his wife about it. She admitted that she had transferred Dorothy but assured him that the school was obliged to refund the money. Mr. Sutton told his wife that he was willing to let Dorothy go to Virginia only if he received a refund from the first school. She wrote the school and pointed out that she had given four months' notice of her decision to withdraw Dorothy.

Once again the school wrote that the contract did not obligate it to refund the tuition, explaining that it had not been able to fill Dorothy's place. Mrs. Sutton wrote a threatening letter. About two weeks later a prominent New York attorney, a trustee of the school, called Mr. Sutton and suggested that they discuss some way to resolve the "distressing matter."

One might have expected Mr. Sutton to sue the school, to determine whether the contract gave him the right to recapture half of the tuition in view of the fact that his wife had given reasonable notice. A prompt settlement might have resulted, since this school was dependent upon parents' support. If the dispute were publicized, it might have been difficult to obtain students in future years. The school's failure to obtain a full enrollment indicated a critical situation.

Neither the school nor Mr. Sutton wanted to go to court. After a pleasant luncheon, Sutton amiably agreed to let the trustee decide the matter: The trustee pointed out that, legally, there was no doubt the contract clearly provided that the school was not obligated to refund the first half of the tuition unless it was able to fill the student's place. It had not been able to do so. Therefore, there would be no refund.

Mr. Sutton had exhibited remarkable "restraint." He had several close friends on the school's board of trustees. If he had chosen to do so, he could have arranged a settlement without even filing suit. But it was clear why he hadn't settled the matter sooner. He was getting back at his wife. She had withdrawn Dorothy against his wishes and had claimed that a refund would be made. Mr. Sutton had been willing to give up half of the tuition just to make his wife look foolish.

On the other hand, if the school trustee had made a personal approach to Mrs. Sutton, the dispute might also have been avoided. Mrs. Sutton probably would have been willing to leave Dorothy in the school for another year. If not, she at least would have realized that the contract did not require the school to refund the tuition. The controversy between the Suttons and the school had little to do with logical issues. Mr. Sutton's quarrel was directed against his wife. The school was little more than a whipping boy.

However, family fights can be susceptible to rational bargaining. A fine example are three teen-agers, children of a labor relations executive, who periodically engage in collective bargaining patterned on the techniques of the labor unions that their father confronts in his profession. Their mother plays the part of family mediator. When any of the children complain that their allowances or prerequisites should be increased, they ask their father for a joint bargaining session. These meetings have become quite formalized. After dinner on the appointed day, the dining-room table is cleared. Their father sits on one side, they on the other. Their mother takes up her knitting and sits, pretending to be preoccupied, at the head of the table.

The grievant presents his demands, explaining why he believes he deserves whatever he is asking. In most cases, the other children support his position. Their father then explains why he believes the request should be denied. A frank discussion ensues, arguments are used, threats are made, and retracted, and an attempt to reach an acceptable compromise is explored. Sometimes their mother will intervene. But often she will sit quietly, allowing an exchange to proceed, sometimes quite logical, at other times, emotional.

In this particular family, it has always been possible to reach acceptable agreements, although in one case, where a child was demanding the right to stay out until dawn after a high school dance, the children were dissuaded from a walkout only by the mother bursting into tears. Both sides were so dismayed by her reaction to their impasse, that the whole issue was avoided by the boy's promise to be home at the usual time.

It is unusual for family dispute procedures to be so highly structured, but in many families factions will engage in frank discussions of their positions and will reach compromises. Where a family is unable to handle its problems in this way, it is sometimes possible to bring in a social worker, a marriage counselor, or some other professional to encourage a dialogue. Often a collateral relative, perhaps one of the grandparents, is able to fill this role on a voluntary basis.

In other families, the intermeddling of a self-appointed conciliator will have a bad effect. In one family, the mother-in-law travels a circuit of the homes of her four daughters and makes

an effort to resolve whatever family problems have arisen since
her last visit. One son-in-law described her technique: "The
old battle ax arrives without warning and makes my wife un-
burden herself of every petty grievance she can remember. My
mother-in-law's visits may be helpful for some of her other
daughters' problems, but it certainly doesn't help this family
very much. I wish there were some way that I could convince
her to stay home."

Not everyone can help resolve a family dispute. It is common knowledge that there are unbridged gaps between generations, so that frequently the "wise old grandfather" is insensitive
to the emotional needs and practical demands of his grand-
children. In such an event he may bungle an attempt to serve
as peacemaker between them and their parents. Unless an individual is quite sure that he can exercise the skills of the
mediator, he should hesitate to insert himself into the boiling
caldron of family antagonism. "He that comes between a husband and wife, puts his head between the blades of sharp
scissors."

Especially between former spouses are fights noted for their
irrationality and trauma. Though marriages normally occur between compatible types no conflict can be more acrimonious
than when couples fall out. In the United States significant barriers are raised against dissolution of a marriage, so that many
persons are locked into a family structure against their wishes.
In such circumstances, they can seldom deal sensibly with their
spouses.

A husband and wife who have agreed to break up are obligated to bargain over the terms of a separation agreement, a
contract that establishes an arrangement between them for the
future, including the distribution of property. A frequent and
significant bone of contention is how much support the husband
will be obligated to pay his wife and children.

Because the separation agreement is an attempt to pre-
determine future disputes, couples may feel obligated to dispose
of every minor forseeable disagreement. Sometimes this preoc-
cupation with trivia will obscure the major issues. They often
underestimate the importance of the support issue. Custody of
the children and the rights of visitation seem vitally important
at the time. Later these issues often recede into the background.

Particular artifacts suddenly become important. Serious ne-

gotiation between a husband and a wife may break down because the wife refused to give up an oil painting of the husband's dog. In one case, the painting itself was worth less than
$100. The dog was worth little more. This impractical desire
to retain some part of the husband's possessions delayed the
settlement for at least two months and probably reduced the
amount of support the wife finally obtained.

There are other more practical problems. The more points
that can be resolved and confirmed in the separation agreements, the less likely that subsequent events will project the
parties into expensive lawsuits. Such seemingly unimportant
matters as the selection of schools for the children, summer
vacations, who will keep the automobile, file the tax returns
and claim the exemption for the children can provide grounds
for future lawsuits. All of these details have the potential of
erupting into bitter disputes if they are not decided at once
and as part of the overall agreement to separate.

If you are involved in such a dispute, and are able to
persuade yourself and your former spouse to engage in direct
negotiations over the terms and conditions of your separation,
how should you proceed?

Follow the basic principles of contract negotiation. Decide
first whom you are going to deal with. What does your opponent
want? What concessions are you willing to make? How can you
get the best possible agreement for the future?

You should decide at the outset whether or not you will
involve attorneys in the preliminary negotiations.

Often the bargaining can be completed without attorneys.
But think twice about this. A woman who has been successful
in milking her husband during marriage may obtain a particularly rewarding settlement from him. But her husband, if he
is aware of his weakness, may decide that he would be better
off to turn the bargaining over to an attorney. You should judge
whether you are likely to do better by bargaining directly, or
letting counsel handle the matter. However, the final agreement should be checked by a lawyer because there are many
pitfalls in the process. A couple can plunge themselves into
trouble by making an invalid or even illegal agreement.

Not always are the parties in agreement that a separation
is necessary. In some situations, the moving party will have to
convince the other that the marriage is impossible.

The most important factor in a marital problem is to understand the other party's situation. What could convince the husband to agree to a separation? How badly does the wife need a continuing income? These are typical of the harsh facts that will control the bargaining. And although both parties usually emphasize good faith, it is necessary for anyone in such a situation to avoid being taken by surprise, and if so, to be able to react quickly and effectively.

In one case, a woman wanted to rid herself of a disappointing husband after five years of marriage. He had been unsuccessful in business and had failed to meet her expectations. She discussed an elaborate vacation trip with her unsuspecting victim. He was going to Europe on business. She agreed to meet him and to spend a month driving through France. A "second honeymoon" she called it. Although the husband suspected that she no longer loved him, she convinced him that their relationship had taken a turn for the better. In good spirits, he departed for Europe.

When he arrived at his hotel in Paris, he found a telegram from her: "OUR MARRIAGE FAILURE STOP AM STORING EVERYTHING MANHATTAN STORAGE UNDER YOUR NAME STOP RETURN CONTACT MY LAWYER STOP SORRY."

The husband was understandably shocked. But Paris beckoned. As his wife had anticipated, he decided to stay and enjoy his vacation alone.

"My husband is a weak man. The best thing I could have done was to open his eyes. By shocking him, I made him realize how hopeless our marriage had become and gave him the courage to accept the idea of divorce."

Sometimes it is the husband who deals the final blow. One wife, returning from a two-week visit with her mother, found her possessions neatly arranged outside the door of their apartment, with the note: "I had the locks changed. Do not bother trying to get in. The apartment is empty. I have asked George to act as my lawyer. He will give you some money if you contact him. I do not want to see you again. The last few years have been terrible for both of us. I am sorry."

This tactic backfired. The wife was so angry that she immediately called a well-known trial attorney who sued the husband for divorce, and within a few years virtually stripped him of both income and property. The husband had badly miscalculated, assuming that his mousy wife would meekly return to her mother, leave him alone, and accept the crumbs he was prepared to offer.

By the time a marriage has reached the stage where both parties find it desirable to separate, it may be too late for rational behavior. How tempting it can be at the culmination of a bitter argument for one of them to proclaim that he will take their differences to an attorney and never speak to his spouse again. Gratifying, but expensive. If you are at such an impasse, you should choke down your rage and unhappiness and agree on the following day to discuss the situation and to make plans for your future. Wherever possible, this is preferable to turning the matter immediately over to a lawyer.

If you are sensible enough to engage in such an effort, approach your differences in a practical way. Where and how will each of you live? Who will have custody of the children? When can your spouse see the children? How much money should be paid to support the wife. Or the children? How will your property be divided? What will your relatives be told? How is it best to break the news of your separation to your mutual friends? Should a divorce be obtained, or can this be left for a later decision?

But when the lawyers are in this picture it then will become their task to laboriously piece together new patterns of life for clients. A couple's intimate knowledge of their family problems is an essential ingredient to any intelligent arrangement of their lives after a separation. However faulty, their knowledge of each other's personality can never be shared completely with an outsider such as a lawyer who is brought in to fight for his client's rights and to negotiate a separation agreement in a hostile atmosphere.

It is often wise for couples to be restrained during this difficult period. Particularly when there are children involved, aggressive acts should be considered, lest they injure the children or create an atmosphere poisoned with anxieties and demands for retribution. The parents' instincts to control the children should not be unleashed thoughtlessly in a marital dispute. It can escalate a mere disagreement into an expensive lawsuit.

Some of the least attractive negotiating moves involve the

use of a child. The most vicious form may be to hostage the child, intending to use physical custody as a lever in the bargaining. In one example, a husband and his attorney discovered that the wife customarily left a five-year-old boy alone in her apartment when she went to the corner for her laundry and occasional groceries. They bribed the superintendent to let them into the apartment, removed the boy, and took him to the husband's parents. They charged the wife with recklessness in leaving a young child alone, and threatened to go to court to obtain permanent custody.

The husband was then living in a studio apartment. He had no intention of taking custody of the child. But the raid gave him an advantage in the subsequent bargaining. The wife was willing to settle for a modest amount of financial support because she desperately wanted to regain custody of her son.

One party will often threaten to claim custody, visitation rights, or some other emotionally charged right involving the children. This demand will then be conceded away for a price.

Separated parents sometimes try to involve their children actively in domestic disputes, thus forcing them to take sides in arguments. Some parents do this unconsciously, because they have a latent need to justify their own positions. This too can be brutal.

But unfortunately it is sometimes an effective technique against the other party.

Even after an agreement is signed and peace has been restored it is possible that new problems will arise over the meaning of the agreement. Here again, you should try to resolve the disagreement rationally, and not let your hostilities run away with your reason.

Tom Baker and his wife Helen separated after four years of marriage. They had one daughter. Their lawyers carefully drafted a separation agreement. One of the provisions in the separation agreement was that Tom would pay the educational expenses of the child.

After they were divorced, the Bakers had minor quarrels, particularly after Tom remarried and found his financial obligations increasingly onerous. But not until their daughter was ten years old, did the Bakers reach an impasse. The girl had been taking private dancing lessons for two years. The dancing teacher advised Mrs. Baker that her daughter had great talent, and suggested that she be sent to a professional school for ballet dancing.

Tom told Helen that he couldn't afford such a school. It would have cost over $900. Furthermore, the expense was not "educational." The Bakers probably could have compromised, except that Tom lost his temper and insulted Helen—with the result that she called her lawyer. The lawyer demanded that Tom comply with the terms of the separation agreement, or that the matter be arbitrated.

Tom and Helen selected a priest to serve as arbitrator. A hearing was held at the parish house. After listening to the attorneys argue the case, the priest requested that he be allowed to retain a consultant to give him an opinion of the girl's talent. The lawyers were amenable to the procedure.

Two weeks later, a well-known dance instructor called Helen and arranged for an audition at his studio. Helen took the girl to the studio. The father was also permitted to attend the session, with his attorney. The little girl danced for the priest's consultant.

The priest called the parties together again. The consultant reported that the little girl was quite talented, but was not certain that the particular course was best suited to her style and temperament. He proposed another school, which was even more expensive.

The priest told the Bakers that he had decided that dance lessons fell within the generally accepted meaning of "educational expenses," but that such expenses had to be reasonable. However, whether the expenses were reasonable would depend on the student's talents, the intended use of the dancing skill, and whether or not the dancing lessons were a part of a fixed educational curriculum. Based upon the consultant's report, the priest was in a quandary over whether the expenses of the school selected by the mother were reasonable and educational. He was not sure whether he had the power to direct the parents to send their child to the dance school recommended by his consultant. Therefore, he urged both parties again to discuss the matter carefully in an atmosphere of amicability and reasonable willingness to agree. He urged them to remember that the most important consideration was what was best for the child.

Helen Baker's lawyer requested a decision on the issue sub-

mitted to the priest. That, said the priest, was the most difficult part of his job. He felt that Mr. Baker should search his
conscience and his pocketbook to see whether he might not be
able to finance the dance instruction. Still, he was unable to say
that they were reasonable educational expenses. But he did not
mean to imply to Mr. Baker that he did not have a moral obligation to try to do his very best for his daughter.

Tom Baker was not given a clear-cut victory. Nor was
Helen Baker satisfied. She could not force her former husband
to pay the tuition. It was not even a satisfactory outcome for
her daughter, who had been tested by a dance expert, and
apparently found wanting.

Disgruntled as the Bakers were, their feelings turned to
rage when their received the priest's bill. As he pointed out, he
was making no charge for his own services, that serving as an
arbitrator was part of his pastoral duties. But he did feel it was
fair to send a bill for $400 to pay the consultant. The priest
asked the parties to agree how this fee should be split between
them.

This created another row, not settled until six months
later, when Helen remarried. Tom paid the entire bill as a
wedding present.

Almost a year after the award of the arbitration, Tom
Baker was still angry. As he pointed out, the priest's decision
was unsatisfactory. Arbitrators should accept the responsibility
of reaching their own conclusions, and not rely upon the expert
opinions of consultants unless directed to do so by the parties.

But I reminded him that the arbitrator never would have
been involved if he had been able to keep his temper and discuss a reasonable compromise with his wife.

In addition to children sometimes provoking disputes between their parents, which are likely to result in agonizing lawsuits unless they can be resolved rationally, they may create
fights between their parents and outsiders.

Often, credit that has been extended to the child on the
parents' guarantee provides a weapon.

A twenty-year-old folk singer wanted bookings. Unsuccessful on her own, she decided to retain an agent. The agent
agreed to advance certain expenses to her so that she could

obtain further training and material for her act. The agent also required the girl's mother and father to sign the contract.

The agent tried to book the girl into night clubs, but found that she was too young. None of the club operators were willing to take a chance on booking a minor. In the meantime, the girl was preparing her songs, taking singing lessons, and buying costumes. She spent advances of over $700.

With no bookings, she decided that her agent was incompetent and told him that she was canceling the contract so that she could retain another agent, her dancing instructor.

"I'm perfectly willing to cancel your contract," the agent said. "Until you are twenty-one, it will be impossible to book you into any of the local night clubs. If you will pay me the money I advanced you, I will give you a release."

"Okay, that's a deal," the girl said.

But payment never came. Finally the agent became impatient with the delay and sold his claim to a collection agency which filed an action against the girl and her parents for the amount advanced, and in addition for the services rendered by the agent and his attorney's fees and costs. Since the girl had no money of her own, the parents now found themselves involved in a lawsuit, and had to pay over $2,000. If you were the folk singer's father, how would you have resolved that dispute?

Resolving Partnership Differences

The intimate contact between business or professional partners may be the frequent cause of disputes, but it can also be manipulated to resolve them as well. The key often lies in the personal relationships between the partners as well as between the partners and their customers or clients. For example, in a law partnership, simply knowing the clients, the problems that brought them to the firm, and the sensitive facts of their relationship, puts a powerful tool into the hands of each party. One often finds clients participating in the settlement of disputes between partners, or the threat of client participation being used to force a satisfactory settlement. Partners should also rummage through their memories and files for information that can be used advantageously. The junior partner of one business venture was able to put pressure on his partner most effectively because he happened to know that the man's wife was demanding large sums of money to refurbish a summer house. In return for permitting his partner to withdraw this money from the firm, the junior partner was able to increase his own interest in the business and eventually to take control.

"It was almost as if John's wife was my accomplice. Her demands for more and more cash facilitated my own aim of gradually buying out my partner."

Also a consultant can be retained to help spell out the facts of life. If your partner seems unrealistic, you might consider bringing in an accountant or business consultant to escalate the pressure. And if that fails, a practical demonstration in destruction may bring your partner to his senses (however, proceed with extreme caution and consider the alternatives of its being used against you): absent yourself from the business as long as you can afford, to show him how much he needs you; take home some of the important files; reassign your own customers or clients to another partner. In short, show your strength, within the partnership context.

However, the resolution process should be based upon a simple fact: The purpose of the partnership is to make money, and money can only be made if the customers and clients are satisfied with the service they receive. Therefore it is essential that there be a continuity of operation. Disputes may turn on entirely personal reasons. This being the case, a frank discussion with your quarreling partner is often the best and most expeditious method for finding a solution. The same compatibility that originally drew you together for business purposes will often reemerge and make it possible for you to make up your differences. Neutral partners, mutual friends, trusted employees, or advisers can sometimes serve as mediators in such a situation.

These informal settlements take place far more often than one would think. Business and professional partnerships dislike washing their dirty linen in public. That is why one seldom hears of partnership disputes.

There is really no justification for partnerships having many disputes because it is quite easy for partners to resolve their differences in advance by providing for most eventualities in a written agreement, and the importance of such an agreement should not be underestimated. By specifying what will happen if various contingencies occur, the partners make their relationship better able to withstand the stress of changing circumstances. Without such protection all our examples would be quite commonplace.

A Chicago law firm had been operating under the same partnership agreement for twenty-five years. One of the founding partners became senile and no longer was able to service the firm's clients. His partners asked him to retire.

"Sure," he said, "I'll be glad to take it easier. As long as I continue to receive my share in the business that I originated, I will cheerfully retire."

"That is not exactly what we have in mind," one of the partners explained. "We think that those of us who do the work should participate in the income. When you retire, your share will have to be reduced."

The old man was adamant. "Then I won't retire. Why should I let you pirates steal my clients and make me walk the plank?"

The old partnership agreement did not give either side much comfort. It merely stated that the partners would share "equitably in the proceeds of the firm, with due regard to client responsibilities and profitability." The other partners pointed out that nothing was said about which partner or partners brought the clients to the firm.

"I wrote that agreement," the old man shouted. "I was responsible for bringing in half of your clients. You men must be out of your minds."

The younger men were perplexed as to how their problem could be solved. Unless they could reduce the founder's income, their own shares would be greatly reduced.

One of their largest clients was a manufacturing company whose president had been sponsored by the firm's founder. The younger partners decided to explain the situation to this president. Three of them met with him and asked him to help.

The president made an appointment with the elderly lawyer, told him that he wanted to try to resolve the impasse. What could he do? The lawyer was frank: "I don't care how large a share I receive, but I want my contribution to the success of the firm recognized."

The president of the manufacturing company understood

the problem. He suggested to the other partners that they insert an amendment in the partnership agreement listing the clients the founder had originated, giving him a small percentage in those fees during his lifetime. Then he organized a dinner meeting, at which the larger clients of the firm honored the old man. His pride was soothed, and the dispute between the founder and his former partners was forgotten.

A particularly bitter fight had broken out between two bachelor doctors who had founded a small medical group. The dispute appeared to involve a difference over methods of accounting. One of the doctors was threatening to take his partner to court. Closer inspection disclosed that the partners were really at odds because of a recently employed nurse. The doctors had been dating their new employee on alternate evenings. Only when one of the doctors married the nurse, was the bookkeeping issue satisfactorily resolved.

Regular partnership meetings at which frank discussions could take place about operating problems would have avoided the blowup that subsequently took place. One small law firm dissolved because one partner refused to introduce his clients to his partner. The latter became convinced that his partner was hiding things from him, and broke off the partnership. He felt quite justified.

"It seemed damned suspicious to me. I told him everything I was doing and didn't keep any secrets from him. Time after time, people would come into his office, people I didn't know and would not meet. Maybe I'm eccentric, but it seemed to me there was something very strange about the way he practiced law."

Sudden surprises seem to cause many of the really bitter partnership disputes. In one case, the shock was particularly acute. An elderly dentist, seeking to retire, executed a partnership agreement with a young man who was to sublet his office and rent his dental equiment in return for a modest share of the profits. Then the old man was offered a lucrative practice at a retirement center in another part of the state. It was necessary for him to have his own equipment. Three days before the younger man was to take over his practice, all the equipment and furniture was moved to the retirement center.

The following Monday morning, when the young dentist opened the door to his office, he was startled to discover an empty room. The young dentist tried feverishly to reach his so-called partner. He had scheduled appointments with three patients for the day.

At first the young man considered suing for damages. But instead he complained to his local dental association, which contacted the older man.

"Sure," the old dentist admitted, "I did exactly what he says I did. I'm willing to pay damages. When I rented my equipment to him, I wanted to retire. But my new job is so good I couldn't refuse. Tell him to figure out how much business he'll lose until he gets his own equipment. Then we can work out a settlement. I would have told him ahead of time, but I didn't know where to reach him."

The young dentist knew it would take him at least a month to buy adequate equipment. He called each of his patients and explained his problem. Most agreed to postpone their appointments. He asked his accountant to estimate how much the delay was going to cost. He filed a claim in that amount, and was paid promptly. The old dentist gave him an additional check for $500, and expressed his sympathy to the young dentist: "You have been very decent about this. I know that you could have sued me or made all kinds of trouble with the dental association. I appreciate your attitude."

An unusual dispute. But it was settled out of court as are most disputes between partners.

Negotiating a Personal Injury Claim

Claims for damages resulting from personal injuries are common. How does an injured person collect?

Let's start with a typical automobile accident.

Your wife is driving your car to the supermarket. She stops abruptly at the entrance to the parking lot. A teen-age girl driving her family car crashes into her from behind. Your wife is thrown forward against the wheel. When she returns home without a purchase, you discover that she has been hurt. She has suffered a "whiplash" injury to her neck. She must stay in bed for a week. Her doctor's bills total $75. You will have to hire a woman to take care of your household, another $90. Your wife is in great pain. She will continue to complain about her neck for several months. What can you do?

You discover that the other driver was covered for liability insurance by an insurance company. She was not injured. How should you go about collecting damages for your wife's injury? The minor damage to your car is no problem. Except for your $50 deductible, the insurance company will pay for that. But how about your wife?

If you decide to sue, how long will it take to recover damages in court? Hundreds of thousands of Americans face this question every year. The answer is often disturbing. Many courts are unable to give a trial to a personal injury claim until several years after the accident. A most conspicuous problem confronting the court system is how to process the many thousands of personal injury cases resulting from motor vehicle accidents. The automobile, when coupled with careless and aggressive drivers, provides our courts with too many accidents and too many lawsuits. Court dockets are clogged with these relatively small personal injury cases, and conventional litigation suffers from acute indigestion.

Is it possible to receive payment by the insurance company without filing a lawsuit?

In fact most personal injury claims are settled directly between the injured person and a claims adjuster who is an employee of the insurance company, even before a formal complaint is filed in court. Insurance companies prefer to deal directly with the injured person for a very practical reason: It saves them money.

A study of persons reporting minor injuries from automobile accidents showed that one out of four injured persons collected his own claim. This was in New York City. In other parts of the country, the percentage tends to be higher.

Who are the people who collect their own claims? Is this something that anyone can do? The researchers found that the higher the economic, educational, and social status of the injured person, the more likely he would try to collect on his own claim. The claimants who seemed most competent to handle their own claims frequently did so.

Many people, particularly the poor and less well-educated, do not know that they can deal directly with an insurance company. Some suspect that the insurance company will be unfair. Others do not know how to proceed. What steps to follow? What risks to avoid? Before an injured person decides to act on his own, he should decide whether he is qualified to negotiate with an insurance company. In some cases, expert help is obviously needed.

Where the injured person is a minor or legally incompetent, the law may even require that negotiations on his behalf be carried out by a lawyer.

In other cases, it may not be clear who was at fault. Under the law of most states, an injured person must show that he was injured as a result of the defendant's negligence, and was not careless himself. A legal contest may be required to determine who caused the accident. When the insurance company denies liability, it may not be feasible for the claimant to negotiate directly with the company. But even here, claimants find that insurance companies often will make some offer of settlement, if only to dispose of the claim and close the file.

But the claimant should decide whether he is personally capable of successfully carrying out negotiations.

Anyone who suffers from a heart condition, anxiety, or other handicap should not subject himself to the inevitable strain. Bargaining takes time. The negotiator must be able to present his case with conviction and force. Where a significant sum of money is involved, the matter should not be handled casually.

Applying the above standards, it is easy to see that not everyone is equipped to handle his own controversies with any reasonable expectation of success. But let us assume that you have decided to take a chance on your own bargaining abilities. What techniques might result in success?

Your objective is to obtain the best possible offer of settlement from the insurance company. You can then accept the offer or refuse, and turn your claim over to an attorney. In this connection, be careful not to prejudice your legal rights should you ultimately decide that the insurance company's offer is inadequate. You should often have a preliminary discussion with a qualified lawyer, asking him to advise you whether there are any hidden dangers in trying to do the negotiating yourself.

A preliminary exploration may guard you against unexpected perils. After your conference you will be able to proceed with a better understanding of the alternatives available to you.

It is also possible to ask an attorney to estimate the value of your claim. Explain to him that you are not asking him to represent you, that you merely want his best judgment as to the fair settlement value of the claim. He may be willing to give you an estimate and to charge you only for his time. If give you an estimate and to charge you only for his time.

Do not be surprised if an attorney hesitates to give you an exact estimate. This evaluation process is highly subjective. Fifty experienced lawyers recently watched a motion picture showing an arbitration hearing of a personal injury case. When asked to estimate damages, their responses ranged from "no recovery" to $8,000. The average award was around $2,000. Fixing a value on a personal injury case is not simple, even for experienced negligence attorneys or claims adjusters.

Nevertheless, it is possible to establish a general target area and, perhaps more important, to determine how much recovery you would consider satisfactory. Most injured persons want a refund of their expenses plus a little bit more for their "hurt." How much more? This is for you to decide.

Or if you are still undecided what your claim is worth, you should approach the insurance company with the intention of finding out what will be their best offer. After you discuss the case with the insurance company, you may be better able to decide how much money you are willing to take for your claim.

Before you even lodge your claim in the customary channels of the insurance company's claims department, you might consider a direct appeal to someone at the top of the corporate structure.

Aim for the generals. Sometimes the president of the insurance company, one of the directors, or an important executive may be persuaded to take an interest in your claim. He may be willing to apply pressure on a lower official. If you or your friends have direct access to such persons, you might approach them. The claims adjuster or the insurance company's lawyer is far less likely to embrace the equities of your claim to his bosom. These men are being paid to resist claims like yours.

Several years ago, the president of a large insurance company told a story that indicates that this technique is sometimes successful. He received a telephone call late one evening from a woman in a nearby town. He didn't know her, but she sobbed out her troubles over the phone. Her husband had been killed in an accident. The president's company was the insurer of the driver who had been responsible for the accident. She said that her husband had been a policyholder for the president's company for over twenty-five years. She had tried to deal directly, hoping that her claim could be settled with her local claims office. She had asked for a fair settlement. The claims adjuster had advised her to retain a lawyer, saying that he was not authorized to pay even half the amount she had asked.

She explained to the president that she was only seeking what her husband would have earned during the next few years. Unless she was able to get a reasonable and prompt settlement from the insurance company, she would be destitute.

The president obtained the name of the adjuster who had refused to negotiate with her. As soon as he hung up, he called the adjuster, rousing him from sleep. Then he called the claims supervisor. He ordered both men to go to their offices at once, to review the file, and to make a reasonable offer to the claimant. As the president reported it, after his agent and claims manager reviewed the file, the adjuster phoned the woman and made a reasonable offer, which she accepted.

It is not always easy to reach such a man. He seldom can be approached through corporate channels, because he is well insulated by organizational buffers. He might read a personal letter. More likely a telephone call to his home or office or a personal confrontation may work. It may be difficult for him not to respond to such an appeal based upon fairness and sympathy.

At lower corporate levels, responsibility to bureaucratic procedures helps to shield officials, making it possible for the "hired help" to turn down legitimate requests. The lesson is clear: Where possible, avoid dealing with the "no-men." It is worth a try. The risk of prejudicing your case, if ultimately you do have to proceed through channels, is slight. This is something you can do yourself. And if you are adept at psychological presentations, those that are devoid of legalities, this may be a self-help technique that will get you what you want efficiently and economically.

Assuming that you are unable to locate any inviting target in the upper branches of the insurance company's hierarchy, you may still file your claim directly with the company's local claims office.

When you seek damages from a claims department, you enter a marketplace. There are some customary steps that ought to be taken. Since these negotiations are often carried out by lawyers, it is sensible to make your own presentation as lawyer-like as possible. Before an attorney negotiates with an insurance company, he usually prepares a comprehensive memorandum covering medical expenses and any other costs that can be shown by receipted bills. These items are called "special damages." You can prepare this information yourself.

In the case where your wife was hit from behind by a teen-age girl, your statement of special damages might read as follows:

Dr. Arthur Ames: 2 office visits, 3 home visits
    (receipted bills attached) $75.00
Drugs 27.50
Travel to doctor's office 7.50
Additional domestic help: Miss Adele Simpson
    (canceled check attached) 90.00
                                          _____
Total $200.00

You might also attach the doctor's description of your wife's injuries, the history of treatment, and his prognosis for recovery.

In other situations, there might be bills for hospital treatment, X rays (attach copies), ambulance service, nursing care, and any other expenses directly related to documentable injuries. Sometimes it is useful to have a medical report from a specialist.

The insurance company will also want to know how long the pain caused by the injuries continued, and how much time from work was lost. Recoveries from insurance companies are partially based on the "pain and suffering" caused by the accident. A personal statement on the degree and extent of such suffering, or even a signed statement from family members testifying how they observed the pain, sleeplessness, and other discomforts caused by the injury will sometimes impress the claims adjuster.

Whatever information you can provide that bears upon

your wife's past pain and suffering, future pain and suffering, past loss of income, future loss of earning capacity, and any other personal loss resulting from the accident should be gathered together and presented to the claims adjuster. Many attorneys prepare such brochures as part of their settlement discussions. There is no reason why you cannot do the same.

In your settlement brochure you might also include your own letter describing the injuries as your wife reported them to you at the time, stating that she stayed in bed for a week, and that you had to hire a woman to take care of her household. (Remember to report your wife's complaints during the period of her convalescence.) Also include a letter from the woman you employed for household duties following the accident. She too would report how much time your wife spent in bed, her complaints, and particularly the pain she complained of while she was there. In this part of your settlement brochure, you are trying to convince the insurance company of the existence of intangible elements of damage. Your statement should be un-impeachable but should make the strongest possible showing of such damages.

Your brochure can be left with the claims adjuster at your first meeting. By presenting your damages in an orderly fashion, you make it easier for him to justify his settlement figures to his superiors.

It is good practice to make a telephone appointment with the claims adjuster, his supervisor, or the highest official you can reach in the claims department. Tell him that you do not plan to retain an attorney until after your discussions with him. Negotiators find the creation of such a "deadline" useful. This is a deadline that is within your control. If you can convince the claims adjuster that you will retain an attorney unless a settle-ment is reached, he is more likely to take the negotiations seriously.

At your first meeting, you should undertake two goals: to establish your credibility and good standing in the community, and to demonstrate that you understand the full magnitude of your rightful claim. Do not attempt to bargain. State your case in a dignified way. Make a subsequent appointment to discuss the company's offer. Tell the adjuster that you assume his com-pany will wish to investigate you and your story in order to establish the justifiable value of your claim.

At the first settlement conference, you may be asked to have your wife submit to a medical examination by the company's doctor. In most situations, this is a reasonable request. But treat the examination as a hazardous encounter. Do not allow your wife to be garrulous during the accompanying interview, or to discuss the accident with the doctor. He is likely to report what she says to him as well as her physical condition.

An elderly gentleman was injured while riding in a taxicab in New York City. He was thrown forward against the partition and had bruised and strained his knee. This had inflamed a preexisting condition, which kept him off his feet for several weeks and required doctor's visits two or three times to his home. About three months after the accident, he asked a lawyer to negotiate with the insurance company. When his claim was filed, the insurance company asked for a medical examination. The lawyer accompanied his client. During the examination, the attorney had to place a telephone call on another matter. When he returned, the claimant was chatting amiably with the doctor.

The following day, the lawyer received a call from his client: "I hope you don't mind," he said. "After talking to the doctor yesterday, I decided there was nothing permanent about the bruises. In fact I'm feeling better every day. I don't want to get tied up in litigation over this thing. Anyway, I called the claims adjuster and he agreed to settle the claim for my medical expenses plus a few hundred dollars for your fee. I hope you don't mind."

Obviously, the man had given away much of the potential value of his claim against the insurance company. But who was to say he was wrong? He did not need the money. To him, his claim was insignificant and he may have been justified in resolving it as promptly as possible.

In some situations an insurance adjuster will come to the hospital shortly after an accident to pressure an injured party into an immediate settlement. Where the victim is badly shaken by the accident, such tactics can be effective. No injured person should settle his claim that quickly. He does not know how extensive his injuries may be. Furthermore, at that stage, the adjuster may not be authorized to pay an adequate amount for injuries. He may be trying to move in quickly for a cheap settlement. The injured person should not permit himself to be rushed.

In our hypothetical case, the insurance company may wish to examine your wife under oath before making an offer. Resist this. An admission made at such an examination may provide the defendant with ammunition to use at the trial. Participate in such examinations only if you have retained a lawyer.

At the appointed date, you should return to the claims manager's office prepared to negotiate your claim. Do not hesitate to bargain. If you have friends or relatives who bargain better than you do, bring them along. This is a marketplace— behave accordingly.

Bargaining over the amount of damages caused by an automobile accident constitutes a relatively simple negotiation. How much is the injured person willing to accept as compensation? How much is the insurance company willing to pay? Although a variety of complex legal and factual issues may ultimately have a bearing upon the primary dispute, the sole object in preliminary bargaining is to determine how much the claim is worth.

You should not waste your time arguing questions of liability with the claims adjuster. If he does not agree that his insured is liable, he will make no offer or an inadequate offer. Your job is to find out how much the company is willing to pay and to try to persuade the adjuster to increase the amount, provided he has the authority to do so. Relevant facts are of course your out-of-pocket costs and the intangible damages that were sustained. Concentrate on these aspects. When the claims adjuster mentions a settlement figure, stubbornly assert that it is inadequate, far short of what would be obtained from such a case in court.

The dialogue might go like this:

"Mr. Jones, even if we assume that the doctor bills were necessary, the highest that I can offer you in settlement is $600. We don't like to pay more than three times the out-of-pocket expenses."

"That may be so but in my situation you have to realize that my wife's injuries were extremely painful. I think I have shown that the pain involved was severe and that it lasted for a long time. I don't see how your company can restrict itself by an arbitrary method."

"Well Mr. Jones, I have told you what our policy is. What do you think would be fair?"

"Five times my out-of-pocket costs would be a minimum figure—$1,000 is little enough."

'I might be able to improve our offer to some extent. But I think you will have to be reasonable. Let me take it up with our home office, Mr. Jones, and I'll be in touch with you next week."

They might settle for $800.

The evaluation criteria of a company claims adjuster is based on what he thinks a claimant could collect if the matter should ever be tried in court. Perhaps the claim would be denied entirely. Can his company prove that its policyholder was not negligent? Or that the claimant himself was? If there is a chance for the company to win on either of these issues, the adjuster will reduce his offer by whatever possibility he sees of escaping liability altogether. Where the claimant realizes that issues of this kind may be involved, he should not be surprised to see the insurance company refuse to make any offer, or to offer only a nominal amount. But usually the claimant is confident of his claim. And here is where the stature of the claimant in his community and his personal credibility are important because when the claims adjuster is convinced that the claimant's testimony will be well accepted in court, he will be impressed by any statement the claimant may make to him in the settlement negotiations.

You should give some thought to the point of view of the claims adjuster with whom you will be dealing. He is not a highly paid official. Your wife's claim is only one of many hundreds that he has to settle. But he has a significant amount of discretion over the price his company will pay, and he is under some pressure to close out files at the least possible expense. This adds up to the fact that the adjuster is motivated to settle cases promptly and at satisfactory figures if he is approached in the right way by a claimant who impresses him as having a justifiable case.

In dealing with the regular claims staff of an insurance company, you should avoid the delusion that an appeal to sympathy will increase the company's offer. Whether or not the claims adjuster "likes" you will have no effect upon the offer, except as to how your personality might impress the members of a jury. The claims adjuster is a professional. He looks at each claim against the background of thousands of others pinned like dead butterflies against the categorical logic of his claims manual. Therefore, uniform procedures and pricing policies are followed, as in the purchasing department of a large department store. The analogy to a market is very apt. Claims managers often explain that they could have "bought" a claim at a lower figure than the claimant ultimately received in court.

The insurance company's initial offer is not likely to be final. Likewise, your original demand should not be the minimum amount you would be willing to take. It is quite customary for both parties to make opening demands and offers that are the outer limits of where they would expect the case to be settled. This leaves room for concessions by both sides during the course of the bargaining.

If the negotiation is carried out in the form of haggling, it is sometimes possible to forecast where the approaching concessions will bisect each other. If this point is below the figure you are willing to settle for, you should abruptly break off the haggling process. Very often, that figure will tend to reach a midpoint between the opening demand and the opening offer. This may not be satisfactory.

However, there is a practical danger in making initial demands too high. If the claims adjuster feels that your demand is so high that it is absurd, he will refuse to treat it seriously.

As one claims adjuster put it, "I will not bid against a figure I believe to be unjustifiably inflated. When a demand like that is made to me, I flatly refuse to negotiate. Nine out of ten times the claimant will begin to bid against himself; he drives his own figure downward in an effort to get me to participate. Once he begins decreasing his demands, I stubbornly resist the temptation of making any offer because sooner or later he'll have reduced his demands too far. If you are bidding against yourself, you have no where to go but down."

Adjusters will sometimes adopt this tactic even when they think the opening demand is reasonable. Then the claimant must be sophisticated enough to force a counterbid at the appropriate time. If the adjuster will not play the game, you have no recourse but to terminate the interview, retain an attorney, and file suit.

When a party wishes to hold the line at a particular figure, there are a number of ways this can be done. One technique is to become stubborn, and doggedly repeat the prior figure. This tactic can sometimes be supplemented by repetitive statements on the justification of the claim. Occasionally an opponent can virtually be worn down although this method is not likely to succeed against a professional insurance adjuster.

Sometimes it is possible to convince the other party that no further concessions can be made. This is particularly likely where a negotiator is speaking for someone else. The company claims adjuster may use this technique in referring to his authorized limit, or to the "reserve" which has been placed upon the case. He may give the impression that he has reached the absolute limit of his authority. There is no reason why the claimant can't use the same technique.

One doctor negotiated a personal injury claim on behalf of his sister who had been injured in an automobile accident. At one stage in the settlement discussions, the doctor told the adjuster that his sister had given him a figure of $4,000 and had not authorized him to settle for less. At that stage in the negotiations, the insurance company had already offered $3,500. This doctor's ploy resulted in an increase of $500. Had his sister really limited his authority? "Of course not," he told me, "but it seemed to be a good idea."

Sometimes one of the parties will give the impression that he is at the end of his patience, or that his interest in continuing further negotiations has waned. Preparations for leaving or terminating the discussions may be made ostentatiously. This is frequently a bluff for both. But there is always the danger that the bluff will be called. The claims adjuster may give the claimant a hearty handshake and show him to the door. Then it may become extremely difficult to initiate further negotiations.

One lawyer uses the "lost briefcase" trick. When he walks out of settlement discussions, he leaves behind an old briefcase. This gives him an opportunity to return to his opponent's office without losing face. Another ruse that can sometimes be used to continue discussions is the "discovery" of new evidence, or a "relapse," or almost any plausible excuse to meet again.

It seldom helps the claimant to prolong the bargaining by scheduling more than two conferences with the insurance company. Insurance companies can wait; in the meantime the "reserves" against the case are invested in interest-bearing securities. Once the claimant has reached a point where he believes he has obtained the best possible offer the company is willing to make, he should accept it or reject it, and break off the discussions.

Collecting Debts

If individuals and companies did not pay their debts promptly, commerce would be impossible. Fortunately, when goods are sold or services provided, the debtor usually pays without delay. There are various techniques used by businessmen to obtain payment within a reasonable time. Some of these methods can be used by individuals as well.

For example, in many businesses the seller will offer a modest discount to those customers who pay promptly. On the other hand, delinquent customers are required to pay cash in advance of delivery. And when a particular customer has been habitually delinquent, the businessman may refuse to continue selling to him.

The prevalence of credit reports is a significant factor in convincing negligent businessmen that punctual payment is preferable. When a business acquires a reputation for slow payment, its credit will suffer.

What can a businessman do, short of filing a lawsuit, when he is confronted with a customer who refuses to pay for delivered merchandise? Most companies usually follow an orderly collection process involving correspondence that rapidly escalates from polite requests for payment to the actual filing of a lawsuit. Here, legal process is used to persuade the debtor that in the long run payment will be preferable to contesting the matter in court.

In some industries, it is customary to include an arbitration clause in every sales agreement. Then, should a dispute occur, the debtor faces a more immediate prospect of having it resolved by an impartial decision maker within the few weeks or months that it takes to bring an arbitration case to a hearing. Often both parties prefer the arbitration process to the courts because they can resolve the dispute privately, economically, and probably more swiftly than would be likely in court.

Are there other techniques that can be used by a party who

seeks to collect on a latent account? There certainly are, and some of them have already been described in earlier chapters. For example, where the validity of the debt is uncontested, it is sometimes useful to be sure that members of top management in the debtor's organization are aware of the delinquency. Copies of collection letters can be sent to the top officials of the other company. If an individual is involved, copies of letters can be sent to his family, to his employer, or to anyone else who has influence over him.

For example, a secretary in a legal office had purchased merchandise on credit far in excess of her ability to pay. One merchant decided to put pressure on her by sending copies of the collection letters to her employer. After two of the firm's partners had mentioned the matter to the secretary, she deferred to the merchant. She paid his bill in advance of many others. She eventually had to apply to a consumer credit bureau to consolidate her accounts, liquidating them on a long-term arrangement. The one merchant, by using his imagination, avoided the delay and inconvenience of joining the general program. He was paid before the magnitude of the situation became clear to other creditors.

Other techniques are used to collect debts. A few would be considered unethical if carried out by an attorney. In some situations, the first time a debtor learns that a judgment has been taken against him in court is when his salary is garnisheed. This can be done by a creditor who is able to obtain an affidavit of service from his process server without the legal papers actually being served on the debtor. Although highly illegal, this so-called "sewer service" sometimes occurs, often when the individual debtor can ill afford the cost of retaining a lawyer to vacate the judgment.

A few collection agencies are experts at using other unethical tricks to expedite payment. Usually, these techniques involve high-pressure methods. For example, an employee of a collection agency may telephone the debtor's neighbors and leave a message requesting the debtor to call concerning the money that is owed. This trick will embarrass and intimidate the debtor and may result in payment. Others may pose as a government agency or threaten police action if payment is not made. Of course, the most blatant of these techniques will only work on an unsophisticated and frightened debtor. But many individuals fall into this catagory.

Whatever the reasons for nonpayment of a debt, collection can best be assured by maintaining a pressure for payment upon the debtor. For example, each firm has its own battery of collection devices. Some knowledge of these techniques is equally useful to the individual who is owed money. An invoice is sent on three separate occasions, followed by a collection letter, followed by an attorney's letter, followed by a summons and complaint. Even without putting the matter in the hands of an attorney for filing a lawsuit, it is possible to put increased pressure upon the debtor.

The campaign need not be limited to correspondence. Telephone calls can be made periodically. Within ethical and legal limits, a creditor need not be restrained in his demands for payment. Sometimes it is possible to humiliate or to threaten the debtor into payment, or to convince him that unless he pays you will implacably pursue him to the end of time. The worst mistake you can make is to permit your debtor to believe that you will not pursue the matter further. In a contest, almost nobody pays voluntarily. Thus, it is up to you to convince your debtor that he has no choice but to make good on his account.

Often a personal confrontation between creditor and debtor will expedite payment. One landlord makes it a practice to appear personally at the door of any tenant who is more than three days late in paying the monthly rent.

"People have a way of putting these things off," he told me. "But when you are standing before them with your hand out, it is hard for them to say no. If I let my tenants get in the habit of paying me late, I would not be able to meet my own bills. It is worth my time to keep after them."

We encounter situations in arbitration cases where payment could have been obtained if the creditor had moved swiftly to find out why it was being withheld and what he could do to expedite payment.

A typical collection case in the textile industry involved two lots of woolen goods, which had been sold by a mill to a finisher. The mill had been paid promptly for the first delivery, but had been refused payment on the second.

At the arbitration hearing, the arbitrators were surprised to

hear the finisher admit that there was nothing wrong with the
second shipment. The finisher asserted that the first shipment
had been of inferior quality. He would not have paid for it if
he had taken the trouble to inspect the goods when they were
delivered. When he discovered the defects, he held up payment
on the second contract in an attempt to get a discount on the
first batch. The arbitrators refused to allow this. The claim
submitted to arbitration by the mill had been based on the
contract for the second shipment, and the finisher was ordered
to pay the full purchase amount. If the sales agent for the mill
had bothered to find out why payment was being refused, he
would have learned about the problem with the earlier shipment. A compromise might have been arranged. In any case
the expense and inconvenience of an arbitration would have
been avoided. It is up to the creditor to find out why he is not
being paid and to try to persuade the debtor to honor his
obligations.

The owner of a fashionable dress shop in Nassau, in the
Bahamas, worried about the delinquent account of one of her
best customers. The lady would not respond to bills sent to
her. Nevertheless, she continued to come into the shop every
week and to purchase expensive apparel. When her account
had become exceedingly delinquent, the owner drew her aside
one day and asked her why she was not paying her bills. The
customer was outraged: "I resent being reproached in this manner. I would think that you would be glad to have such a
person as myself for one of your customers. You must appreciate that the amounts involved are trivial to me. Please do not
mention this to me again. I'll pay you when it is convenient."

The proprietor was astonished at the woman's attitude and
allowed her to leave without discussing the matter further. At
first, she considered writing a collection letter, demanding that
the entire account be paid before further charges would be
honored. But two evenings later, she happened to meet the
lady's husband at a dinner party. She told him about the situation and asked his advice on how to approach his wife.

"I know exactly what the problem is," he said. "My wife
dislikes paying bills out of her household account. As regards
these monies, she is extremely penurious. If you approach her
trustee [a local solicitor] you'll find that the matter can be set
straight without much delay. She has ample funds to meet her

obligations. But by some strange quirk in my wife's nature, she fanatically guards her own personal account. In short, you're hunting the fox down the wrong lane."

The owner of the shop thanked the gentleman and on the following day approached her customer's trustee. "Certainly, I'll have a check for you within the week," the representative promised. And so he did. From then on, whenever this lady made a purchase at the shop, payment was requested from the trustee and honored without further ado. All that had been necessary was to discover why the lady was withholding payment. The secret was a personal eccentricity. In other cases, there may be different reasons.

Professional Fee Disputes

Professional fees present special problems to the professional and his client or patient. Such disputes are common. For one thing, the professional seldom executes a signed agreement with his client before carrying out the work. It is hard for him to forecast how much time will have to be devoted to his client's problem. Instead, he completes the work, totals up the number of hours expended on the project, and sends a bill.

An architect does most of his work in his office. The client sees only the finished drawings. In the case of a lawyer, regarding legal research, the client may have assumed that the lawyer already knew the law.

All of these factors converge upon the moment that the client receives the bill. "My God!" he roars, "this is highway robbery. This man must take me for a fool."

And no amount of explanation will ever convince the outraged client that the professional has not grossly overcharged for his services.

If a client seriously objects to a fee, a professional is often tempted to withdraw his bill. But where a client has engaged in fee practices that are patently unfair, it may be appropriate for the professional to stand his ground and insist upon payment.

In a recent arbitration, a doctor had served as an expert witness for an insurance company. The company protested his bill as excessive. The doctor persisted, asserting that his bill was fair. No agreement could be reached, but both the doctor and the company were willing to arbitrate. A hearing was held, at which the doctor presented his time records. The company produced evidence regarding the custom and practice of other medical experts. A panel of arbitrators, including a doctor, lawyer, and accountant upheld the doctor's position.

Afterward, the doctor ruefully admitted that he was unlikely to be asked to serve again as an expert witness. "But I proved my point," he asserted. "I only charge what I am worth."

The doctor might have been well advised to compromise his claim. But he had no aspirations to become a "full-time professional witness," since most of his income came from practicing medicine at a local hospital. It was a matter of principle.

What can you do when you believe that the professional's fee is too high? Certainly you can refuse to pay and explain to the lawyer, architect, doctor, dentist, or other professional exactly why you think you are being overcharged. If the professional is unwilling to compromise, there are special avenues for expediting a settlement. You can get in touch with the appropriate professional association. Or you may want to bring the matter to the attention of the man's business associates. The professional's reputation for fair billing practices is valuable to him. He is particularly susceptible to such pressure points.

The most successful technique usually is an attempt to induce the professional to reduce his charges voluntarily in order to avoid the adverse publicity and trouble that could be involved in collection procedures. More than other businessmen, professionals dislike having to spend their time and energy collecting fees from their clients. This is the trump card in the professional equation and you should not hesitate to play it.

One doctor told me: "I have never refused to reduce a fee when asked to do so by a patient. Many years of experience has convinced me that the time I spend arguing about fees is wasted and is not worthy my attention. If I can't persuade my patients that my fees are reasonable, well, I am glad to reduce them."

Another technique sometimes used to force concessions is a threat to file a malpractice claim. This seldom is successful. A malpractice claim tends to harden the positions of the parties by introducing into the situation the professional's insurance carrier and its attorneys. Do not attempt this tactic unless advised to do so by an attorney.

As a professional, what are you to do if your client refuses to pay at all? Ordinary collection procedures are sometimes useful, and a telephone call can be particularly persuasive, because your client will listen with respect. By explaining exactly how the work was done, and why it was necessary to perform each particular function, you can often persuade your client to pay the fee.

In most cases, it is far better to involve yourself personally in this collection process than to turn the matter over to a collection agent. The agent starts with several strikes against him. He does not have your prestige. He is not familiar with the details of the services rendered. His presence may close the door on rational discussion of the differences between you and your client.

Sometimes you will find it useful to offer to submit the reasonableness of the charges to some impartial person, and to be bound by whatever decision is reached. This can be done quite informally. For example, a dentist may say to his youthful patient: "I do not want to be unfair. You show my bill to your father. Tell him how many appointments you had in my office and describe the work I did for you. Let him be the judge. If he says my bill is too high, I will reduce it."

Of course, it would be a mistake to make such an offer unless you are convinced that no impartial person could deny the justice of the claim. You should be assured also of the impartiality of the person named. In one case where a dentist made an offer along such lines, he was shaken to discover that the boy's father felt his fee to be far too high and recommended that he take one-third of the amount he had charged.

Professional fees are unusually difficult to collect because of the ephemeral nature of the services provided. It is clear that most professionals would prefer to have such matters resolved privately, either through a process of mutual concession or through the intervention of an impartial arbitrator. Almost none of these claims has to be taken to court, since neither party wants his affairs subjected to public scrutiny.

The best way to avoid disputes over fees is a thorough discussion between professional and client before the work begins. It is the surprised client who screams the loudest about high fees. If the professional had taken time to outline exactly what would be involved in the work to be done, the controversy might have been avoided in advance. Clients can sometimes be prepared for a high fee by periodic progress reports: What is the professional doing? What still has to be done? How much more is the work likely to cost? When an unexpected development in his situation takes place, the client should be advised and told about how it will affect the work. In this way, there will be no surprises, and the client will have less cause to complain when he receives the final bill.

Protection in Home Improvements and Construction

In recent years, the home improvement and construction field has been particularly marked by controversy. Homeowners are approached by contractors and signed up for ill-defined jobs. Often these improvements result in much larger bills than the homeowner expects. Or the quality of the work is such that he is unwilling to make payment. Construction projects generally have been subject to rapidly rising costs, and contractors have cut back on the quality of their work to stay within contract prices. In addition, there are disputes over delays, the cost of change orders, poor performance, and other issues that arise under contracts.

The responsible factors in the industry are concerned; various government agencies are showing an "alarming interest." And undoubtedly, many sharp practices exist. Nevertheless, it is fair to say that many of these disputes could have been avoided if the homeowner had only taken the time to be sure that he understood exactly what he was buying. A number of steps could be taken to avoid controversy.

Contractors have typical pressure points. They're in a competitive business and need capital for oncoming projects, which makes them aggressively collection-minded. Builders who are short of capital often are forced to compromise a claim for less than its value. As an owner you should obtain accurate information on the builder's financial status. (Many an owner has been disappointed when construction had to stop because the builder did not have adequate funds to pay his subcontractors.) Often the architect on the job, or, in some cases, the engineer, is in a position to help you exert pressure on the builder. In most cities, the building construction industry is a community unto itself, where every contractor is well known; his reputation is peculiarly important to him.

Litigation between contractors and owners can be extremely expensive because of the technical nature of the problems. For example, when a case turns upon the quality of materials provided for a job, or upon the accuracy of an engineering survey of subsurface conditions, the proof can be technical and time-consuming. Litigation is particularly slow for all parties and expensive in attorney's fees. Almost any other way would be preferable.

I remember a situation where the builder of a ski lodge in Vermont got into difficulty because he lacked experience in the finishing treatment of a prestressed concrete foundation. The lodge jutted out over a stream running along the edge of a ski trail. The owner was adamant that the surface be perfect. Unfortunately, the concrete had cracked because the finishing treatment was not correctly applied. The owner held back final payment. At first the contractor said that it would cost several thousand dollars to completely refurbish the exposed concrete. This he refused to do.

After a week or two, the contractor realized that if he were going to recover any part of the final payment, he would have to satisfy the owner. For the first time, he began to consider how the concrete could be refinished to the owner's satisfaction. He persuaded a consulting engineer to drive up from Connecticut to inspect the job. Fortunately, the engineer provided a technical solution that made it possible to strip the cracked surface with chemicals, and then by quite a different process refinish the entire surface.

"I might have received a few bucks more in arbitration," the contractor told me. "But then again, I might not have. And anyway, I hope to build many more houses on this mountain. You don't get new customers by arbitrating with your old ones."

An impartial survey of a contested job would provide a bargaining tool by which a construction dispute could be compromised. This may be a better way to handle these problems than any form of adversary process. The architect is able to serve as a mediator or fact finder. The American Institute of

Architects suggests that the architect be given an opportunity to decide such issues before any steps are taken to resolve disputes by arbitration or in the courts. Where the architect is impartial between the parties, this often is a useful approach.

"Once the work is under way," one architect told me, "I try to help the parties. I see myself as a referee, assisting in the solution of any difficulties that may come up. By then, I know more about their project than anyone. Usually they look to me for accurate informed decisions, sometimes for solutions."

In large construction programs, contract specifications writers may work for months or even years preparing the details of a project so that both parties know in advance exactly what is expected of them, and exactly what standards they must meet. Everything is described in meticulous detail, even the catalogue numbers of hardware to be used on the job.

If you are building a house you should do exactly the same, and the architect should be required to provide comprehensive detailed plans. With proper forethought and detailed plans, it should be simple to avoid the experience of one young man who engaged a contractor to build a prefabricated weekend house in a small upstate New York community. When he drove up from New York City to take possession of the house upon its completion, he discovered that there was a drop of five feet between the doorway and the lawn. He spent his first weekend searching for large rocks in nearby fields so that he could enter his house without pulling himself up with his hands. Back in the city, he looked at his contract. Sure enough, the contractor was not obliged to build steps.

Chapter 5

HOW PROFESSIONAL EXECUTIVES RESOLVE DISPUTES

Business provides a fertile laboratory for anyone who wants to study working models of dispute settlement procedures. And these procedures had better work. The urgent need to make a profit motivates business managers to design efficient ways to resolve disagreements.

Corporations are exposed to many potential disagreements. They risk conflict when they sell their product, purchase material, services, and supplies, contract with executives, and when dealing with employees and the consumer public. They deal with contractors, retain lawyers, accountants, and experts of many kinds. They hire salesmen, arrange for dealerships, and let out franchises to sell the goods they manufacture. They buy and sell real estate and rent buildings. Every business agreement contains the risk of disagreement over its meaning.

This chapter will consider some of the ways that professional executives, operating in the competitive and complicated arena of business, manage to avoid destructive controversy.

First of all, the interplay of power determines the overwhelming majority of business disputes. It would be naïve to think that the courts or privately devised systems of dispute resolution, such as arbitration, play a major role in this type of dispute settlement.

When, for lack of caution or for inadequate advice, a dispute arises between executives, and one of them has not guarded against such an eventuality by retaining the right to

decide the matter in his own interest, he engages in a number
of well-known bargaining techniques. In various ways, he tries
to persuade his opponent to make attractive concessions in order
to reach an agreeable compromise. Each situation will call for
a unique bargaining equation. Or as one industrialist put it,
"I see my weekly game of squash and my daily round of business as one and the same. The rules are different but each
requires me to be alert and aggressive, yet subtle."

The executive negotiator follows the same basic rules that
have been discussed in other settings. He analyzes the problem,
tries to select the most appropriate adversary, and aggressively
carries out a carefully planned campaign.

In addition, he can try bluffing his opponent or exposing
him to his own top management. And since bargaining techniques are not covered as part of his academic preparation, he
learns by practice.

Even if a settlement cannot be reached through negotiation
or through the use of bargaining pressure, it may still be possible to persuade the other party to submit to binding arbitration. Arbitration clauses are often inserted into contracts, because a businessman would rather put his case before an experienced arbitrator than submit to the burden of court procedures. Nevertheless, arbitration should be thought of as a
last resort, only preferable to litigation cases where settlement
proves to be impossible.

Unilateral Power—a Business Ideal

Where possible, a businessman uses form contracts that
have been tested in action and are slanted in his favor.

In moving into a new apartment, a tenant will probably
be asked to sign a form lease by the landlord. If he looks at
the lease carefully, the tenant will see that the landlord has
tried to guard himself against disputes that are likely to arise.
For example, the landlord will protect himself against the possibility that the premises might be used for illegal purposes. A
form lease will usually give the landlord the right to terminate
the agreement if the tenant fails to pay rent or fails to abide
by the other obligations of the lease. Most provisions in the

lease will be designed to guard against future disputes, usually backed up by the landlord's carefully guarded right to evict in appropriate cases.

In many situations, form contracts reflect the fact that one of the parties is stronger and has the power to decide the terms and conditions of the relationship. But the party that writes the contract may not always have enough bargaining power to get his own way.

The business of an advertising agency had been dealing with the building manager of the office building. Most of the provisions of the lease had been agreed upon. Both parties thought that they had achieved a satisfactory deal. Then the representative of the advertising firm turned his attention to the uniform tax escalation clause (the rent would increase automatically with the real estate tax on the building).

"I don't believe in this kind of clause in principle," he said. "It's the landlord who should be on the hook for increasing taxes. Otherwise he has no motivation to seek an abatement. My management won't agree to this clause. Also, we have been reviewing our plans to decorate the executive offices and find that it's going to cost us about $5,000 more than we anticipated. These two items have to be considered together."

The building manager first tried to talk him out of his position on the escalation clause. Finally, he had to admit that he was not authorized to change the provision. The escalation clause had to be uniform throughout the building to comply with mortgage requirements.

"Well then, I'm afraid the deal is off," the business manager said. "We might have been able to go along for the escalation clause. But the additional cost in renovating the premises disturbs me. I'm afraid I can't recommend the lease to my firm."

"What if we agreed to pay for some of the costs of improvement? Would that solve our problem?"

"Yes. An additional $5,000 for improvements would make the difference."

The lease was signed on that basis. The business manager told me later that the president of his agency had masterminded that final trade. "We had a good lease, and we knew it," he said. "But we did think the landlord was being inflexible in

insisting upon a tax escalation clause for his own convenience.
Our president thought that the building manager might buy
off this problem with an increase in the improvement money.
He was right."

When a businessman has a strong bargaining position, he
will strive for the exclusive right to interpret the terms and
conditions of the agreement. Wherever possible, he will retain
this power.

For example, when selling a franchise to distribute his
product, or when arranging for a long-term supply commitment, the negotiator for a dominant corporation will demand
a right to cancel the contract. The most effective commonly
used technique for avoiding litigation in contract disputes is
the exercise of overwhelming power converted into unrestrained
discretion.

This "big power" technique may be used with the cool
efficiency of a butcher's cleaver: "If you wish to do business
with us, you must do business as we desire." Contracts with
businessmen who do not agree are terminated.

A candy manufacturer entered into a three-year exclusive
franchise agreement with a department store. The franchise
cost $6,000. Although the candy company's standard form con-
tract established the terms and conditions of the agreement, the
department store demanded the right to cancel the franchise
in the event that it did not meet a minimum profit level. The
candy company was very eager to sell franchises because it was
suffering from a shortage of operating cash. It had to agree. The
department store also demanded the right to locate the candy
franchise anywhere in the store. The candy company agreed
to this too.

As long as the franchise was located on the main floor, it
easily met the minimum figure. But when the store moved the
candy counter to the second floor, gross receipts plummeted.
Profits from the candy franchise no longer exceeded the minimum amount. The department store notified the candy company that it was exercising its option to cancel, and demanded
repayment of the original option price.

The candy company refused. It claimed that the store had
not been making a good-faith effort to sell candy. The transfer
of the candy counter to the second floor had caused the reduced
sales volume. The form franchise agreement required the store

to "use its best efforts to sell such products." The contract also included an arbitration clause, which covered disputes arising under the contract.

At the arbitration hearing, it soon became clear that the candy company had no defense. The contract gave the store the right to select the location of the candy counter. The arbitrator had no difficulty in awarding the department store the entire franchise price. By its superior bargaining position, the store had protected its interests.

In most contracts, where bargaining power is roughly on balance, the parties, after identifying issues that may arise during the course of a contract, can devise some method for determining them privately or leave them to be decided in court.

But what about disputes that are not based upon an existing contractual relationship between parties? Disputes may erupt during negotiations. In such an event, the stronger party often issues an ultimatum to the weaker. It is not unusual for large companies to maintain inflexible policies regarding certain clauses in contracts they negotiate with suppliers or customers. Sometimes, these clauses can be oppressive. We see absolute unilateral power in the following example.

The president of a small manufacturing company in New Jersey told me about a dispute he had lost against a large defense contractor. The facts of the controversy were perfectly clear. He obtained a contract to provide titanium struts for a weapons assembly. One of the dimensions set forth in the purchase order had been wrong. The purchasing agent admitted that the specifications were faulty. Nevertheless, the contractor refused to pay for the struts when they were delivered. He returned them to the subcontractor and gave directions how the defect could be corrected. The corrections would cost about $32,000, not compensated under the contract.

This was too much money for his small company to write off, particularly since it wasn't his fault. The president paid a visit to the purchasing agent. "How do you have the gall to ask us to correct your own mistake? I have a good mind to dump this whole thing into a federal court. It's absolutely unfair, and you know it. My company can't afford this. Isn't there something you can do for us?"

"Look," the purchasing agent said. "I won't put this in writing and I will deny it if you quote me. But the work that your company does for us is pretty small potatoes. There are dozens of subcontractors. Each year you have been getting a larger share of what's available. I admit that on this we made a mistake. But I can't admit that officially without bringing down all kinds of repercussions upon my head. I just cannot afford to open up that particular can of worms on such a small item. Let me put it this way, if you will accept your losses and bail me out, I will see that you make it up on other contracts. But if you make an issue out of this, you will never get another piece of business from this company. We don't have to do business with you. The price of doing business is to ride along with us when we need you. You get the picture?"

For the price of redoing the titanium struts on this small contract, the subcontractor obtained favorable consideration for several future orders, which more than made back his losses. "That's the way it goes when you deal with the big fellows," he told me philosophically. "Win a few, lose a few. But you don't win any if you start rubbing their noses in their own dirt."

Just recently in California, the general counsel for a large defense contractor described his company's solution: "We try to generate enough power so that no subcontractor finds it worthwhile disagreeing with us. With our subcontractors, we can write our own ticket. That is what the federal government does to us. The contract officer can sign a slip of paper that blocks us from collecting hundreds of thousands of dollars. We have to play the same game with our subcontractors."

Neither the government nor powerful corporations are eager to submit issues to any tribunal. More practical is the exercise of arbitrary economic power, the most luxurious private solution.

What to Do About Contract Ambiguity

A contract is a plan for the future. To the extent that the transaction involved is important, you ought to make sure that the plan protects your interests and resolves every likely contingency that might result in a fight. Here is the time to get expert advice, to be careful, and to reach out for help.

Unfortunately, this is exactly the time that too many individuals act stupidly by signing any contract that is put before them. Nonetheless, businessmen, particularly those who deal in large amounts, are quite opposite in their approach. As this section will show, they emphasize meticulous contract preparation, the participation of experts in planning, a reliance upon well-tested form provisions, and the use of arbitration clauses to handle "open" items.

As with partnerships, a lesson to be learned from big business is the importance of reaching agreement on all the details of a business arrangement in advance of signing the contract. This cannot be overemphasized. Similar attention should extend even to purchase orders or any transaction under which someone is to provide goods or service in accordance with specifications. In preparing a contract, detailed specifications can sometimes be supplemented by samples to show exactly the quality that will be required. But this is tricky business. A product can vary from a sample and yet be perfectly merchantable. A testing laboratory or bureau of standards report is often less relevant than the business judgment of a businessman. Be careful not to tie up the other party by requiring unrealistic contract standards.

In huge corporations any important transaction will involve professionals to work out the complicated details. These people will often be lawyers and accountants.

For example, in preparing a stock prospectus, a bond indenture, or a corporate merger agreement, teams of corporate lawyers will draft legal documents that run hundreds of pages and attempt to cover every possible contingency that might arise out of the transaction. A task force of lawyers will spend months on such a project, identifying possible problems, making sure of their facts, and incorporating all of their information and expertise into a document that will govern every step of the transaction.

This process culminates in a mass of documents, to be signed by the parties, a monumental investment in professional time. Thousands of potential problems have been eliminated by careful planning, and the entire venture has been meticulously programmed for maximum security and minimum risk.

A relatively simple stock underwriting will require the preparation of fifty separate documents for signature by one party or the other at the closing.

There is a Wall Street story that when one of the upper windows of the Chase Manhattan Plaza building popped out during a storm, sucking hundreds of documents for such a closing from the desk of the law partner in charge of an important corporate merger, the unfortunate man clapped on his hat, went home, and retired from the practice of law forever.

Form contracts are often used by businessmen and lawyers because they have been pretested in the courts and approved by lawyers and trade associations for use in similar transactions. Businessmen should check with their own trade associations to see whether particular forms have been designed especially for their use. A contract that has been approved by a trade association is more likely to be problem-free than one that is freshly prepared by an individual businessman or his lawyer. Many lawyers are aware of this and use printed forms that have been widely accepted by their client's industry. Even when the client is given a typewritten contract for signature, he will often find many "boiler plate" provisions from the printed forms current in the trade.

Once a contract is in force, and a dispute arises over an ambiguity that was not apparently intentional, it sometimes helps for the parties to call in the actual draftsman of the contract. Ask the man what he intended. If the draftsman is not obviously committed to one side, he may be able to explain the intended meaning of his language and the reasons for his choice of words. But do not overestimate the usefulness of this technique. The draftsman's memory is susceptible to selective recall. He will seldom remember a fact that prejudices his employer's position.

Information concerning similar language in similar contracts can have persuasive value. Businessmen are impressed with facts relating to customs and practices in their industry; where feasible, attempt to persuade your opponent that your position is acknowledged by the industry. Where reason fails, you are thrown back upon the power equation and you must exercise economic force to obtain satisfactory results. At that point, the best tactic may be to brush aside the ambiguity and to bargain directly for a settlement. Businessmen often "agree to disagree," in order to find an alternative solution to their controversy; it is important not to let yourself get bogged down

by extended quibbling over the meaning of a particular contract term.

Sometimes a show of impatience can be used to jolt the
negotiations into a more rewarding vein. In other situations, a
switch of negotiators will be needed; the president of the company may take over from the lawyers. In the same way, an individual should realize that persuasion must sometimes give way
to raw bargaining.

For practical reasons some eventualities cannot be guarded
against in the contract. For example, one party may be reluctant to discuss an issue in advance and the other party may overlook it. Or both parties may anticipate the problem. But they
may be unable to devise a formula to dispose of it in advance.
Before going ahead with such a contract, however, the intelligent negotiator will make sure to remain flexible to bargain in
creative and unexpected ways. Perhaps an example will show
how such a situation may occur.

Two small companies formed a joint venture to develop a
new scientific technique for commercial uses. Company A would
provide the technological expertise, company B would contribute manufacturing and marketing skills. At the outset, they
were able to define their respective rights and obligations in
general terms only. They could not accurately fix the respective
percentages they would share in net profits should the venture
prove successful.

One negotiator suggested that they use vague language,
providing that profits be "shared in accordance with the relative contribution made to the success of the venture by each
party." This was acceptable to both companies. Having intentionally created an ambiguity in the contract, which might result in future disputes, they also inserted an arbitration clause.

The joint venture prospered. Then an engineer sued both
companies, claiming that the joint venture was violating his
patent rights. They settled with him. Now a problem arose. The
accountant for the joint venture, having paid the settlement
amount, asked how the payment should be charged. Should
both companies participate in the cost of the settlement?

Company B pointed out that it had relied upon the other's
statement that the technique did not infringe existing patents:

It should not have to contribute to the settlement. Company A claimed that the settlement was a normal business expense and should be charged against the joint venture and that a fifty-fifty contribution would be fair and equitable.

The top executives of each company met with the accountant to see if agreement could be reached. For more than three hours they argued over the issue. Finally the accountant who had been trying to persuade them to compromise lost his temper. "You men are wasting your time and mine. If you can't agree, why don't you recognize the fact. After all, you have an arbitration clause in your agreement."

"That's right," said one of the executives. "If we can't agree, we can always arbitrate. But that would be expensive and we would have to bring in our lawyers. I'll tell you what, why don't we hold a mock arbitration, with our accountant acting as arbitrator. Perhaps that will help us to reach agreement."

That is exactly what they did, each presenting his arguments, with the accountant sitting at the head of the table. When they were through, they asked the accountant what would be his decision.

"No thanks," he quickly said. "I'm not going to decide against one of you. But you both heard the story. Don't you think that you can come to an agreement? After all, you have a good business going here. It would be a shame to let it all go down the drain. Why don't you split the difference between you?" Company A would pay 75 percent, company B, the remaining 25 percent. "If you don't agree, you are going to wreck your business. This way you can continue to make money."

The two companies accepted their accountant's suggestion, and since then have made many thousands of dollars in profits.

Bluffing—a Negotiating Technique

Although the ideal situation for a businessman is to have enough power to make demands that will have to be accepted by his opponent, we have seen that such power is not always available. But there are alternatives. Often he can achieve satisfactory results by the threat of taking some detrimental action.

The business negotiator first estimates exactly how much each party has to gain or lose in the particular conflict. Then he studies his opponent's characteristic behavior, whether he is a "hawk" or a "dove," whether he customarily reacts logically or emotionally. His aim will be to convince his opponent that he will be forced to accept the concessions offered. The nice name of the game is "negotiation." An uglier name may be "extortion." This is brinksmanship. Where his opponent is convinced that he will not hesitate to carry out such an action, he may decide that the better part of valor is to make the required concessions.

Even in run-of-the-mill cases, a businessman will do almost anything to avoid litigation. This can be a source of weakness.

A Harvard Business School task force recently studied dispute settlement from the viewpoint of the businessman. Based upon hundreds of interviews, their report confirmed this reluctance to litigate, at all levels of involvement.

Many years ago, Judge Parker of the United States Circuit Court remarked upon the lengths to which businessmen were even then inclined to go to escape litigation: "Business corporations are willing, as all of us know, to suffer almost any sort of injustice rather than face the expense, the delay and the uncertainties of litigation."

This is not to say that businessmen acquiesce in the loss of profit opportunities. On the contrary, they aggressively confront the other party in negotiations. Their techniques are efficient and methodical.

Some professional negotiators have adopted a theory that it pays to be as unreasonable as possible to the edge of convincing their opponents that it is impossible to deal with them. Seen this way, conflict negotiation is a form of salesmanship. The negotiator is "selling" his opponent on the advantages of making concessions.

The basic transaction is always played out in the mind of the opponent. Therefore, the professional negotiator is very much interested in his opponent. Where his opponent is overly sensitive to the economic costs of controversy he is fair game for a convincing bluffer.

Bluffing can be risky. A New York City landlord held a corner building, a shabby tenement, on a block that was being assembled for a modern office building. If the new building was designed around his lot, the potential value of his property would plummet.

He did not know when the builders would have to decide

whether to design the building around him. The builder was constantly threatening to "lock up" the design. So far, he had not believed in the threat. By diligent sleuthing, the landlord established a contact with an employee in the architectural firm that was preparing the preliminary drawings of the new office building. Through this contact, he discovered that the critical date would be in about three months. In the meantime, the demolition of the other buildings on the site would be carried out.

The problem facing the landlord was to persuade the builder to offer the highest possible offer. If he made the first move toward reopening negotiations, the builder might take it as a sign of weakness. Thus it was necessary to take the initiative without seeming to do so. As the weeks went by, the landlord wondered what to do. Finally he decided to draw the attention of the public to his problem, hoping to persuade the builder to make one more try at buying him out.

By this time, the other buildings on the site had been demolished. The landlord covered his small corner building with signs: "This building is a monument to independence," "Why are they tearing down our city?" and finally, "This building is the last vestige of independent ownership." Naturally, the newspapers gave this a big play. Within twenty-four hours, the landlord received a call from a representative of the builder, and was able to reach agreement.

In these negotiations, the landlord was able to establish his reluctance to vacate his building. The landlord not only received the full price he was asking, but moving expenses and a new and better location as well.

Brinksmanship of this kind can sometimes be rewarding. As one real estate speculator told me, "My finest deals have been when I was able to convince the other party that I was half crazy, that I sincerely believed that the property had the value that I was asserting. My worst deals have been when I tried to appear rational and to establish values through logic and comparative figures. I am not selling property. I am selling convictions."

Memorials to other small landlords who challenged builders in the same way and lost are on display in any large city. The lonely small building embraced by huge new developments on each side may sadly tell such a story.

Not all such confrontations are so dramatic. One of the tenant owners in a luxury apartment house wanted to build a sun room on his terrace. When he told the board of directors what he planned to do, they refused to permit it.

He took the position that he should have the right to do what he wished with the terrace. He called the president of the corporation: "You people have no right to stop me. I want you to know that if you don't reconsider your decision I'm going to take this building to court."

"Let me discuss the matter once more with the Board," the president suggested. "It doesn't make sense for tenants in a cooperative building to sue their own company. It will be expensive for all of us. Let me find out what the other directors want to do."

"I'll give you thirty days to give me permission. Then I am going to bring in my attorney. This is important to me."

When the board of directors met the following week, the attorney for the building was also present. "What are our rights?" the board asked him.

"I think you can stop him," the attorney said. "But this question does not often arise. Most tenant-owners abide by the decisions of their representative board. Do you think he will really sue?"

"Who knows this man?"

"I've only met the gentleman on a few times," said the president. "But I think he means it. When he talked to me, I had the feeling that this was so important to him that he probably would sue. And I know he can afford it."

"What will the other tenants do?" asked the lawyer. "Do you think others will build structures on their terraces?"

"I don't think so," replied the president. "There are only eight apartments that have terraces. I doubt that this will set a precedent."

"Well then," concluded the lawyer, "why are we contesting it? I can't recommend spending the building's money to stop something that most of the tenants don't care about. If he is really going to sue the building, why wouldn't it be better to let him build his sun room."

The directors agreed, under the threat of a lawsuit, that it would be prudent to reverse themselves, and to permit the tenant to build his sun room.

Some bluffs are just naturals. In a dispute involving an airplane lease, the lawyers had reached a stalemate. The question was whether a corporation had to pay for the rental of an airplane that a former vice president had rented for his private use.

The attorney for the company had prepared a detailed and convincing legal memorandum showing that it was not within the authority of the vice president to rent an airplane, that the lease had not been approved by the corporation, and that the rental firm should have known that the plane was being used for personal business. From a legal standpoint, the evidence in favor of the corporation seemed convincing.

However, the rental firm's attorney knew that the stock of the company was controlled by a prominent industrialist. He also knew that the erstwhile vice president had been the industrialist's son-in-law. He asked for a meeting. There he presented a copy of the lease, signed by the vice president, and the rental records and receipts. The lawyer demanded payment in full.

Counsel for the corporation lawyer recited the principal parts of his memorandum, which proved that the vice president had no right to rent a plane on behalf of the company. He pointed out that all of the trips had been to resort areas—East Hampton four times, Cape May twice, and once each to Lake George and Manchester, Vermont. One of the trips had even occurred after his discharge. Counsel strongly recommended that the claim be denied, and asserted that no court in the country would hold his client liable.

When the claimant's attorney demanded an opportunity to examine the defendant under oath, the industrialist abruptly concluded the meeting. That afternoon, the corporation's attorney telephoned the lawyer for the rental firm and offered a settlement. The controlling stockholder did not wish to admit in court that his former son-in-law had taken his company for the price of eight joy rides. The creditor's lawyer was skillful enough to parlay some elemental psychology into a prompt settlement.

Some bluffs came in big packages. One young company achieved a critical and early victory by suing another company that had dared to manufacture a similar device.

The new company was still manufacturing its product in

the garage of one of the founders when it discovered that another small company was producing the same product in a nearby town. The president of the new company wanted to ignore the competition. He thought that money might better be invested in new facilities and advertising.

"No," said his lawyer. "You should gamble for big stakes in this one. If your product is everything you say it is, you can always get money to expand your plant and increase your market. But unless you have an exclusive right to manufacture and sell your product, other companies are going to jump in before you really get started. What you must do is to smack down the first company that tries to compete with you. Your patents are valid but you have to establish the fact that you are willing to fight for your rights."

"Taking this company to court is going to cost all the money I have," the president complained.

"Nevertheless, it has to be done. There are probably other people getting into this field we don't even know about. We have to scare them away, otherwise we're going to lose our exclusive rights."

A lawsuit was filed to protect the patent rights of the company. The lawyer made sure that news of the litigation was carried in business and trade publications that would reach any likely competitors. The company's news releases emphasized that it was prepared to take on every businessman who would try to manufacture their product. Before it was settled, the lawsuit had cost the company $20,000 in court and lawyer's fees.

Now the corporation makes profits in millions of dollars and licenses its patent rights to other manufacturers.

Shopping for the Best Deal

One technique customarily used by professional negotiators is the multiple approach. There is no requirement that only one individual be approached in a controversy or only one individual initiate discussions.

In a dispute over the price of merchandise, discussions might begin between the purchasing agent and a salesman, and simultaneously between the production manager and a marketing executive, and also between the two top executives of the companies involved. If an advantageous concession can be obtained at any of these levels, it can be accepted. One warning: All executives who participate in such a multiple approach should guard against committing the corporation to a solution that might be less advantageous than one received by another executive. The campaign should be coordinated.

Particularly where a company is poorly coordinated, exploring settlement possibilities at several corporate levels at the same time—probing for the most satisfactory terms—may provide the best combination of concessions or may locate a weak spot in the opponent's armor. If there is a choice, the professional negotiator selects the weakest executive.

Multiple bargaining must be handled delicately. When the executives compare notes, one of them may conclude that an attempt has been made to circumvent him.

In one case a dispute over the quality of a large order of synthetic textiles was permitted to drag through three years of litigation because one executive—the division manager for the mill that produced the fabric—felt he had been left out of the negotiations. Time after time, the company's attorneys would come to this man and ask whether they should settle. He always refused. Finally, after judgment had been received against his corporation, he admitted that he had not expected to win.

"We all knew that the production run was not up to contract standards. If the purchaser had come to me directly, early in the game, we would have given him a discount on the order or even replaced it. But the first I heard about it was when they filed a lawsuit. If you let people blackmail you, you might as well get out of business."

When the lawyers pointed out that the main office in New York knew about the dispute long before the case was filed in court, he replied, "That doesn't make any difference. I'm the man they should have dealt with. My division sold the material. The problem should have been brought to me, not to our New York office."

The importance of identifying the proper target for negotiations cannot be overemphasized. Experienced lawyers are particularly aware of this fact.

One lawyer was shocked by the size of a printing bill submitted in connection with the corporate prospectus. It was $800 more than he had anticipated. He was embarrassed to show the bill to his client.

He knew the president of the printing company and invited him to dinner. After dinner, while he and the president were enjoying coffee and a cigar, he raised the subject of the bill. The president was not very interested. He said he would prefer that the matter be discussed with the manager of the printing plant, promising "My company will do whatever is fair."

The following day, the lawyer called on the manager. "Your president was at my house for dinner last night, and I mentioned this bill to him. He told me to come to you to have it adjusted. I think it is about $800 too high. Will you see that the change is made?"

A day later he received a new bill, reflecting the reduction. He did not know whether the manager even mentioned it to his president. Quite possibly, the manager would have found it embarrassing to bring up. However, by careful selection of his negotiating target, and a little manipulation, the lawyer accomplished exactly what he set out to do.

Understanding the Issues

Lying beneath the problem of locating an appropriate target within the corporation is the sometimes more difficult task of identifying the issue in dispute. Sometimes the dispute may involve a simple disagreement over the appropriate price of an article or for a service.

Where a dispute involves objective standards, it is possible for parties to arrive at some logical compromise. At other times, the reason for the dispute is obscure. Then it is necessary for one or both parties to investigate the situation more thoroughly, seeking a comprehensive understanding of the controversy, and to establish a plan of action.

A young attorney for a large manufacturing corporation reported a situation where the main problem was to analyze the dispute. The employees in one of the company's smaller plants filed a petition with the National Labor Relations Board to be represented by a union. The president of the company wanted to know why. Could something be done about it? He told the young lawyer to talk to the plant manager.

When asked what was wrong, the plant manager replied that he couldn't understand it. He had always been able to talk to his people—"They knew my door was open at any time." Salaries were on a level with most other plants in the area. Supervisors were in touch with with him every day. Production was up. So far as he could tell, the employees were 100 percent with the company.

"Why did they file the petition?" the young lawyer asked.

"The only thing that I can figure," responded the manager, "is that outsiders are getting to them. Tell the president not to worry. I can take care of this situation. I always have. I intend to talk to the workers tomorrow. I'll give them the facts of life and let them know that if they don't drop this foolishness, the plant can be moved somewhere else."

The young lawyer knew that any such speech would only result in further trouble among the employees. He telephoned the president of the company, asking permission to study the matter further and take whatever steps were indicated.

After the lawyer had talked to a number of supervisors and other executives in the plant and had made a survey of the conditions on the factory floor, he concluded that there was insufficient communication between the production workers and the front office. He persuaded the manager to embark on a crash program to improve the facilities. He visited the employees in small groups to hear their complaints.

The supervisors received a briefing about the representation election, and were told what they could and could not do. Many of them reported complaints and bad situations existing on the factory floor that were causing discontent among the workers. These differences were resolved promptly and the supervisors reported that the feeling toward the company was improved.

By the time of the election, the production workers were much more favorably motivated toward the company. By a small margin, the voters rejected the union. Before the lawyer left the premises, he had designed a personnel program for the manager to follow. The manager had been shocked to discover that he did not know what was going on in the minds of his own men. From then on, he cooperated fully. With the help of a well-designed program for communication between the employers and the supervisors, the morale and productivity of the branch continued to improve.

In many such cases, an investigation will disclose an entirely unexpected reason for the other party's point of view. Sometimes the trouble is totally personal.

A Broadway producer was unable to rent a particular theatre. The owner refused to talk to his agent. Only six months before, the producer had ended a long run of a profitable musical comedy at the same location. He could not understand why the landlord would not discuss another lease—he knew that the property was free and that the landlord had no other immediate prospects.

Suspecting a personal problem, he asked his wife, an expert at digging out the latest Broadway gossip, to find out what was wrong. Within a few days, she told him the reason for the impasse. Two weeks earlier, the producer had been lunching at Toots Shor's with a well-known actor and an important financial backer. He had failed to notice the landlord across the room. The landlord believed that he had been snubbed—he had told mutual friends that he would never again do business with the producer.

Having discovered the problem, the producer decided how to resolve it. Once again he called upon his wife. She immediately asked the landlord to dinner and to the opening of an important play. The landlord accepted her invitation, which gave the producer an opportunity to lavish attention on him, to convince him that they were still "close friends." An advantageous lease was signed a few weeks later.

"If my wife hadn't been able to find out why the poor slob was avoiding me," the producer said, "this difficulty might have continued for years. He's known for his paranoic hatreds. I never would have known why he had it in for me. Now I have my play in the right theatre."

Many disputes involve good-faith misunderstandings over facts or legal obligations of the parties. But sometimes controversies are created by less worthy factors. A party may know that he ought to pay a claim, but still will refuse to do so.

One saloonkeeper frankly acknowledged to a secondhand bar equipment supplier that the purchase price was due and owing, but blandly asserted that he intended to withhold payment until the following year so that he could deduct the amount against taxable revenue—which he anticipated would literally flow from his new operation. The supplier was furious, but decided that it was not worthwhile suing him. The confident bartender was accurate in his business judgment—his bar made profits. The supplier waited seven months, and was then paid.

A purchasing agent for an office copying-machine manufacturer almost destroyed a relationship with a new supplier because he was afraid to admit that he had made a mistake.

One of the company's products, some relatively simple office machinery, included a cast-iron bar that served as an axle. Only the ends of the bar were exposed to view, but these ends had to be smoothly polished. The rest of the axle was concealed under a cover and was left unfinished as it came from the casting operation. For a number of years, these bars had been purchased from a foundry that delivered the castings ready for assassembly into the machines. Then the foundry was awarded a large government order, and was unable to continue supplying the purchasing agent's firm.

In reporting this to the agent, the salesman of the foundry disclosed that, "Every once in a while, when we were too busy, we subcontracted your job to another foundry nearby. Why don't you get in touch with them and see if they want your business?"

The purchasing agent followed the suggestion. He thought even better of the idea when, on calling the second foundry, he was told that they could do the work for him at a slightly lower cost.

The manager of the foundry was eager to obtain a new customer. He did not expect to have any trouble filling the order. He had been making these rods for years and assumed that he could meet the order in the same way. The order was placed. And the purchasing agent let the word get around his office that he had found a way of cutting production costs.

What happened was something quite different. When the first shipment arrived, it was discovered that the ends of the metal bars had not been polished. They were as rough as the rest of the casting. The purchasing agent protested. Only then did he learn why the price was low. The original foundry had been performing the polishing operation. Now it was up to his company either to finish the job, which it wasn't equipped to do, or find someone else who could.

That "someone else," the purchasing agent decided, ought to be the new foundry he was dealing with, and the work should be done at the quoted price. The solution was the only one that would save his face.

The foundry didn't see it exactly that way. They had not contracted to do the finishing, and they saw no reason for doing additional work without additional compensation. The purchasing agent refused to authorize extra payment, so the matter went to arbitration. It was a simple matter of contract interpretation. What was the new supplier obliged to do?

First, the manager of the foundry explained how the purchasing agent had called up and asked him to produce several thousand axle rods, "just like the ones they had been buying from the former supplier." The foundry had quoted a price and agreed to supply the "same rods they had been making." The purchasing agent had seemed delighted with the price. The foundry manager then produced the purchase order, which contained the arbitration agreement. He asked for payment in the full amount.

Next, the purchasing agent testified. He had taken one of the polished axle bars with him when he signed the order blank. He admitted that the purchase order did not specify that the ends be polished. But he stated that he had intended to order "by sample." He asked that the cost of polishing be deducted from the purchase payment, or that the work be completed.

The arbitrator asked him whether he had specifically told the foundry to polish the ends. The purchasing agent could only say that he had shown the manager a finished rod. When the arbitrator asked him whether he had "simply assumed that the foundry would polish the rods," the attorney for the purchasing agent whispered to his client that it might be wise to try settle the case. But by that time the foundry was not interested in a settlement. The lawyer's hunch was correct, if late.

The arbitrator held that the foundry had no legal obligation to polish the rods and ordered payment to be made, with 6 percent interest. Swallowing his pride, the purchasing agent was able to arrange an agreement for future requirements at about the same cost his company had been accustomed to paying.

How the Businessman Uses Formal Arbitration

Executives will frequently insert an arbitration clause in a contract. Such a provision is intended to protect the company from the expense and delay of having a dispute determined in court. Some of the cases I have previously described show how this process is used.

The reader may not be entirely familiar with arbitration. It is a method by which parties can design their own tribunal. In drafting business contracts, parties often try to avoid the inconvenience of conventional litigation by agreeing to arbitrate disputes in regard to the terms and conditions of the contract. This does not mean that every disagreement has to be arbitrated. Most disputes can still be resolved by negotiation. But if the parties are unable to settle a particular issue, the contract provides arbitration as a private remedy, preferable to litigation.

When two businessmen file an arbitration case with the arbitrating agency of their choice, they are sent a list of arbitrators who are experienced in their own business. From this list, they strike off names that are not acceptable or those not believed experienced enough to hear the case. Then each party indicates its preference for the remaining names. These lists are returned to the administrator, who appoints an arbitrator. The arbitrator is the highest mutual choice of the parties. A convenient date is then set for the hearing.

The parties prepare for the hearing in somewhat the same way that they would prepare for a court trial. But it is often possible for them to agree upon many of the facts in advance so that they will not need to take the arbitrator's time to submit evidence not in controversy. Where the relationship between the parties is reasonably good, it is possible to present the evidence informally.

The witnesses for each party explain the facts of the case to the arbitrators. The arbitrators are given broad powers to supervise the hearing, and maintain decorum and a businesslike atmosphere. Usually there is no need to have a transcript taken. This reduces the formality of the proceedings, and the cost.

In arbitration, the aim is to persuade the arbitrator. Legal rules of evidence are not applicable. If the arbitrator is a businessman, familiar with the customs of a particular industry, it will be easy for business witnesses to communicate with him.

Terms can be used that would be meaningless to a jury but are a part of the day-to-day jargon of the trade. A businessman will feel at home in arbitration because he is with experts in his own business. (It is not unusual for executives to sit around a table discussing a controversy that arose in their own business.) He feels in command of the situation.

Tactics are similar to those used by salesmen. The quality of a product may be in issue. One side will be trying to sell the product to the arbitrator. The other side, like any purchaser, will try to convince the arbitrator that the value of the product is less than the seller is claiming. Late delivery, cost of changes, changing circumstances, failure to agree to the transaction—all of these controversies are quite familiar to businessmen. And when it comes to convincing an arbitrator on such issues, the businessman will feel as competent as any lawyer. Arbitration is tailor made for the businessman.

In arbitration it becomes extremely important for each witness to establish his credibility with the arbitrator. The witness must convince the arbitrator that he knows the industry. But beyond this, he must establish his good faith, his reputation in the industry as an honest man. Again, these are familiar ideas for the average businessman.

Hearings are held at the convenience of the parties as well as of the arbitrator. This fits into the busy schedule of the merchant, whereas litigation is difficult to schedule and tends to disrupt a business. Sessions are often held in the evenings or on weekends. Only when a party is attempting to delay, will the arbitrator refuse to grant requested adjournments. Nevertheless, the arbitrator, often volunteering his time, is anxious to get on with the matter. He has no motivation to see the procedure drag on. He will be impatient with the party that introduces irrelevant evidence or makes repetitive or unnecessary arguments. Participants in an arbitration should move ahead expeditiously.

We have seen in these pages that the arbitrator's award is subject to very limited review, and that he had a great deal of discretion. Therefore, it is not advisable to argue with him or challenge his rulings. He cannot help but be impressed by the party that cooperates with him in his attempt to ascertain the truth, but he will not be impressed by courtroom histrionics, which may well irritate him.

The presentation of a case should be designed for the particular arbitrator appointed to hear it. If the arbitrator is not a lawyer, principles of law must be stated in simple, compelling terms, and in the language of the trade. Procedural objections should be presented in a commonsense way. Most parties find it prudent to have a lawyer represent them at the hearing. But many lawyers are unfamiliar with arbitration. Some forget that they are not in a courtroom and clutter the proceedings with technical procedural objections. Where possible, it is advisable to retain a lawyer who has had substantial arbitration experience.

Experts feel that the preparation of the facts is the most important aspect of handling an arbitration case. Witnesses must be prepared with particular care for hearings. In the free flow of testimony, the badly prepared witness may easily blurt out an admission or inconsistency that could destroy a case.

In one recent hearing, the purchasing agent for an electrical contractor volunteered that he had already offered to pay 90 percent of what the claimant was asking. His attorney argued that the statement should not be admitted into evidence. But the arbitrators had heard it. It probably increased the possibility that they would render a high award.

Arbitration has its particular applicability in business. Where parties want to submit their dispute to an expert in their own business, they generally will use arbitration; where there is a continuing relationship between parties, which they can't afford to rupture, they will provide for arbitration as a last resort to decide their disputes; where there is a practical need for a prompt and final decision, businessmen often arbitrate. Arbitration may not be a magic remedy, but laymen who are inherently impatient with complex judicial structures, see it as a preferred substitute for the courts.

It is possible to misuse arbitration by trying to turn it into a system that is just as prolonged and expensive as litigation. The process can be delayed and frustrated. Most lawyers know these techniques. During the selection of the arbitrators, it is possible for a party to refuse to agree to the appointment of an arbitrator from the submitted list. It is also possible to postpone hearings by claiming that either the lawyer or the executive is engaged in other important matters, or to ask for adjournments in order to prepare further evidence. By dragging out the hearings, and by making it difficult to schedule them, a party can delay the final award for many months.

I know of one case involving a large construction project where one of the parties took every opportunity to frustrate the procedure. Over six hearings had to be held because that party insisted upon submitting irrelevant data and testimony in an attempt to create delay.

Finally the arbitrators issued an ultimatum, "Gentlemen, we have listened very carefully to every bit of evidence you have cared to submit. Now it is time to complete your case. We will meet every day until your case is closed. There will be no more adjournments, no more postponements, and no more delay."

The following day the case was settled. The respondent was convinced that the arbitrators meant what they said and would push the case through to an award. He decided that there was no more to be gained by delaying the process.

When an administrative agency is not involved, there is even more likelihood of a party being able to block progress. Some arbitration clauses provide for each party to appoint an arbitrator, with the two arbitrators appointing a third. There is no great compulsion upon the respondent to appoint an arbitrator or to participate in the appointment of the third arbitrator. Furthermore, if the party does not wish to schedule a hearing, or to appear at one, it is very difficult for the other party to require attendance. That is why more and more contracts provide for administration of the procedure by a professional organization.

A Seattle builder told me about an experience with one of the informal arbitrations. He wanted to collect for some work he had done in building a small warehouse in Seattle. He looked at his contract and discovered the old-fashioned arbitration clause. He appointed his attorney as his arbitrator, and wrote a letter to the other party asking him to appoint an arbitrator as well. When he received no reply, he called and received the following response.

"Why should I appoint an arbitrator? I have no interest in paying you. Your claim is completely false. I've paid you everything I owe you."

The contractor discussed the situation with his attorney. He was told that by going to court, it might be possible to have an arbitrator appointed for the builder and then to have the two arbitrators appoint a third. "How long would it take?" the contractor asked.

"It is a cumbersome procedure and one that I have never had to use," his attorney told him. "Why don't you try letting me handle it? I may be able to bully this fellow into some sort of settlement. In the long run, it will probably be less expensive for you than going through this other process. Next time, you ought to use one of the standard arbitration forms recommended by your contractors' association. They have a procedure to force the other party to arbitrate."

The attorney wrote to the warehouse owner, threatening to sue him. It resulted in a conference between the attorney and the debtor.

"You have no right to sue me," said the debtor. "There was an arbitration clause in the contract."

The attorney had the last word: "But you refused to arbitrate. My client can file suit against you, and we intend to do it. If you don't want me to proceed, we had better settle the matter right now."

On that basis, a settlement was reached. After deducting his legal fees, the contractor received almost half of what he was owed.

Chapter 6

MODERN TECHNIQUES FOR DISPUTE RESOLUTION

Litigants are not anchored to the court system. They have a right to invent their own procedures, to dismiss the safeguards provided by the courts and to expedite their litigation. This chapter will describe some of the innovations and techniques that are being devised, which will be used increasingly as parties seek efficiency and speed in the handling of their disputes. These techniques are available to the individual who wishes to handle his own controversy.

The very fact that a party suggests an imaginative means for resolving a dispute may have a good effect upon his adversary. A suggestion that the matter be disposed of informally or by the intervention of a mediator, by fact finding or arbitration, may jog an opponent into continuing negotiations toward a successful conclusion.

A vice president of an insurance company, in praising one of his claims adjusters, put it this way: "His major advantage is his ability to improvise, depending on how he sizes up his opponent. He has the gift of versatility. Once he told me he had discovered over fifty different ways to handle claimants and their attorneys. I can believe it! I am amazed at how quickly he can find a way to close out his files."

Negotiators, lawyers, business executives, mediators, and ordinary people who get involved in an argument, all have a genuine interest in learning how to improvise new techniques for bringing a controversy to a conclusion. In fact, anyone who becomes involved in a dispute can profitably spend a few mo-

ments trying to devise a plan of action to jolt the other party
into a settlement or to precipitate a prompt and satisfactory
resolution. As one executive told his general counsel, "I don't
give a damn how you do it, but get this problem [a dispute with
a supplier] solved!" Many people feel the same way about their
own controversies. No matter what, they want them solved.

Sometimes, the primary problem is to obtain evidence that
can be used to persuade an opponent to make an adequate offer
of settlement. Dramatic photographs, videotape recordings of
eyewitness statements, and statistical data can often be used for
such purposes.

But how about those situations where the courts do not
provide an adequate remedy? For example, some poverty
communities have come to regard courts as hostile and useless
for day-to-day disputes. For certain kinds of problems, neighborhood mediation and arbitration systems can be established,
and complaint systems can also be created in other settings
where the parties either are not willing or able to submit the
matter to court. An example is the voluntary review systems
which have been established by some industries to give customers, suppliers, and dealers a fair hearing procedure on contested
claims.

Improving Dispute Settlement Systems

Sometimes whole industries will discover that particular
kinds of disputes are occurring with epidemic frequency and are
not being handled efficiently in the courts or under an existing system. Then it makes sense to take a penetrating look at
the problems and see whether an improvement can be made
in how those disputes are being handled.

A young shop steward in a small local union in the Mid-
west became disenchanted with the formal labor arbitration
system that was being used in the factory where he worked. He
happened to meet the owner of the company and the president
of his union at a Community Fund Drive luncheon. They were
soon discussing the problem. They all agreed that the situation
had deteriorated. Labor arbitration hearings had become too
legalistic, had lost touch with the operating problems of the factory floor. Hearings were being held in a courtlike atmosphere.
Both parties were represented by local trial attorneys. A tran-

script was made of every hearing. Briefs were filed. All apparatus of litigation was present. "Why don't we simplify the procedure?" the shop steward suggested. "My guys are constantly complaining about how long it takes to get a decision. And how can the union afford this situation?"

"Sure," said the manufacturer. "There isn't any reason we can't take this into our own hands. Our differences ought to be worked out on the factory floor. Why don't we agree on a better system? Come to my office in the morning and we'll talk about it."

Next morning, the union leaders met with the owner and other officials of the company. They designed a system of "instant settlement" as follows: If a grievance were to be raised by a shop steward, a meeting would be held on the following day to decide the matter. If the parties could not settle their dispute by agreement, an umpire would be called in for the following day to decide the case—three local arbitrators agreed to serve as umpire on twenty-four-hour notice. There would be no lawyers, no formalities, and no written opinions. When the umpire had heard the case, he would tell the parties his decision. The hearing would be held in the plant conference room.

After talking with some of the workers and getting the approval of his shop stewards, the union president shook hands with the employer: "You have a deal. Now let's see how it works."

The number of grievances in that company has decreased. The workers feel their problems are treated promptly and sympathetically. Grievances are presented by a shop steward, with the help of the union president. The personnel director represents the company. Most grievances are resolved without any need to bring in an umpire. Even when parties can't agree, they have been able to dispose of problems within forty-eight hours. The shop steward who suggested the change is now an executive in the company, in charge of industrial relations.

More effective systems are frequently suggested by business executives and, where they resolve important disputes, top management is likely to reward the man who made the original proposal.

A situation occurred that made it necessary for the parties to design an entirely new system in a complicated dispute involving a foreign operation. Two major mining corporations found it possible to obtain a prompt disposition by relying heavily upon the judgment of outside experts. For tax reasons, it was necessary to establish the underground rights of the companies in a virgin mineral deposit field. Each organization had acquired surface leases. Each company had some data as to the subsurface potential of the area, but not enough for an accurate allocation. How could this material be pooled to establish an appropriate formula?

A young engineer suggested that an attempt be made to expedite a resolution. He was authorized to try. First he spent a week studying his own company's data. Then he met with the head of operations of the other company.

"I have been reviewing the allocation problem," he said, "I don't see any way that an agreement can be reached between our companies unless we share our information and cooperate in trying to find an answer. If we have to decide this in court, it won't be settled for years. Our lawyers are not even certain that the courts will hear the case. Why can't you and I design an engineering solution to this issue."

The other company was agreeable. So the two engineers met together and designed their own system. Each company prepared a memorandum covering its own data. These were thereupon submitted to an impartial consulting firm. (Within two months, the data had been processed. A well-organized report, containing all of the summarized material, was ready for presentation to the corporate engineering departments.)

Each company was given two weeks to review this material. Then they met in a joint session with the consulting firm.

The impartial engineer then explained each step of his calculations. Although the company engineers, from time to time, disagreed over the weight given to particular factors, they became convinced that a meticulous effort had been made to appraise the data, and that the consultant had acted in accordance with sound engineering practice. Finally, both companies accepted his report and agreed to abide by it for tax purposes. Neither the court nor formal arbitration was involved. There was no oral hearing. Neither party had to retain counsel. The impartial engineering consultant predigested the information. The parties were then able to resolve their disagreement scientifically, assisted by the impartial engineer. Much of the cost, adversary bickering, and red tape were removed from the process.

As one engineer said, "Here we have the engineer's ideal of litigation. Gentlemen, I show you the future."

Often, it is not the parties that devise new and more efficient procedures. It may be a lawyer, a management consultant, or a disinterested third party who makes the suggestion. Whatever the source, innovation in dispute resolution can be a boon to the contesting parties.

New Ways to Communicate Disputed Facts

If Abraham Lincoln returned to Illinois and entered a modern courtroom, it is likely that he would find the atmosphere congenial. The authority and function of the judge, the selection and use of the jury, and the tempo and organization of the trial itself would be familiar to him. Arguments of counsel, couched in customary legal jargon, would make him feel at home. Court attendants, clerks, bailiff, spectators, and even the court reporter laboriously transcribing the testimony would seem familiar. The passing centuries have left the courtroom much as it has always been.

Substantial change in court procedure is unlikely. The courts are reluctant to change, committed to traditional judicial customs, and protected by law from imprudent innovations. Nevertheless private parties can decide their disputes without resorting to the formalities of the court system. They can experiment with modern technologies to dispose of contested cases more quickly and economically.

How can a confrontation of the facts be arranged more promptly? How can the facts and argument in dispute be presented for decision more efficiently? New methods are available for those who wish to use them. New systems of communication are at hand.

Facilities for audio-visual conference calls are already available in many cities and can be rented at a reasonable cost. It may already be old-fashioned to require contesting parties to travel thousands of miles in order to meet together in the same room. It may be practical to bring witnesses and advocates together via electronic connection.

One psychologist chided me, "The methods used for settle-

ment of human disputes are incredibly crude and archaic. Why
do you require a total confrontation? In an up-to-date business,
complicated information is transmitted electronically. Why are
you lawyers still shackled to the live witness and the hearing
room?"

A party can deliver the testimony of a witness in California directly to a settlement conference or hearing in New
York. Witnesses can be examined before a video tape recorder,
or through a telephone conference call, perhaps on an audio-
visual circuit. Parties themselves can move about the country
interviewing their witnesses on video tape, complete with cross-
examination, with the entire record to be played back later
when the parties are discussing settlement or presenting their
case to a decision maker. The reliability of these devices has
been greatly improved. Attorneys know that transcripts are
subject to error. Video tape would be more reliable. Particularly in disputes that involve complicated marketing data,
statistics, or other evidence, the use of computerized information will certainly reduce the time that must be spent by the
attorney processing a case. Individuals involved in disputes
over market prices or consumer rates can utilize the computerized information kept by industry.

Voluminous documents need no longer be shipped across
the country. The same documents could be communicated in-
stantaneously by direct wire connection. They can be mini-
aturized. Paper work can be streamlined by transporting voluminous exhibits on tape or punch cards. Whenever paper
work is expedited or reduced, the cost of processing a case is
cut.

Sometimes lawyers feel that they must laboriously prove
the authenticity of documents. Much of this effort could be
eliminated by agreement between the parties, or by the avail-
ability of certified Xeroxing process or some other expedited
method for stipulating the authenticity of original documents.

A New Jersey engineer who had a tape recorder in his
family automobile at the time of a bad smashup in which his
wife and mother-in-law were injured, made a recording of his
conversations with the other driver (including an apology for
causing the accident), the officers from the highway patrol, and
two eyewitnesses. From their beds in the hospital on the evening

of the day of the accident, the injured women recorded their versions of the accident and described their pain and suffering.

The tape was played to the insurance company's claims adjuster several months afterward and, according to the engineer, helped in obtaining a prompt and favorable settlement. Local rules of evidence would exclude such material from a trial in court, but for purposes of settlement, a taped recording of contemporaneous eyewitness statements may have a great impact on the opposing party.

In the same way, it is often useful to take photographs of accident scenes, property damage, or other sites that are relevant to a factual dispute. Leading trial lawyers are alert to their probative value in court. The individual claimant should not forget that the impact may be just as great in settlment discussions and should not fail to invest in photographs in appropriate situations.

In one case, an elderly man fell on the sidewalk in front of a bar and broke his hip. He told his attorney that the heel of his shoe had caught in the curb. When the attorney visited the site, he noticed a number of places where triangular pieces had broken away from the curb edge, presumably because beer barrels were delivered to the adjacent premises. One of these holes was deep enough to take the heel of the shoe, and might have caused the accident. The lawyer arranged to have a picture of that portion of the sidewalk, with a shoe actually stuck in the hole.

A lawsuit was filed against the city, and was settled years later. The lawyer who handled the case feels that the photograph was vital because it helped fix the theory of his case in the mind of the city's attorney. It would otherwise have been very difficult to prove that the injured man fell exactly where he said he did, or that his fall was caused by the hole in the sidewalk catching his heel.

Rights Without Remedies

Sometimes you will discover that there is no way to assert your rights in court even though your claim can be justified. Either you cannot afford the courts or the courts are not appropriate for the particular issue, or the rights involved are not recognized by the law, or for some other reason a new remedy will have to be devised.

Once again, it will be up to you to figure a way to gain your objective, out of court. Either you will have to find someone to put pressure on the other party, or you will have to organize a group of people with similar interests, or you will have to find some other solution.

First, let's consider the problem of the person who just can't afford to file a case in court.

"What do I care about contracts? I don't have any money, and I never will." These are the comments of an old man on the subject of contractual obligations. A third-year law student, working with a legal-aid program, had been asking him about a contract he had signed. He was an indigent, but astute Bostonian. He realized that the other party could not collect money from him. He was judgment proof.

Nor could he afford to sue another party, even if his claim was valid. The enforcement of a legal remedy, which requires a willingness and ability to go into court, presents so many difficulties to some individuals that their right to sue may be valueless. The expense and irritation of taking a case to court may seem overwhelming.

This is particularly true of the poor. Many jurisdictions have established small claims courts to provide simplified tribunals. In New York City there is a night court in which individuals who have claims for less than $350 can have them heard by an arbitrator—a lawyer who volunteers his services. The individual can present his own case. There is no need to have a lawyer in this court because the procedure is extremely informal.

Another kind of facility developed by the Office of Economic Opportunity is a neighborhood arbitration system. For example, one such system in Cleveland, Ohio, is available for disputes between slum tenants and landlords. These disputes may involve evictions, unpaid rent, bad maintenance by a landlord, improper behavior by a tenant, and other similar problems. A tenant union is organized to represent the tenant. A contract is signed with the landlord, under which he agrees to have disputes arbitrated. Individual tenants are delighted to have a simple yet effective remedy for their disputes.

One landlord who operated an apartment development with two hundred families was having trouble with a gang of teen-age vandals who were wrecking lighting fixtures, breaking windows, and painting graffiti on the hallways. He called a meeting of the tenants and explained his problem. Some of the older tenants offered to organize a tenants' association to try to deal with the boys and their parents. The landlord provided them with a meeting room, and refreshments. "After all," he explained, "I have an interest in seeing that this problem is solved."

The tenants' association was formed and a grievance committee appointed. One by one as the vandals were identified the boys were called before the committee. One boy refused to attend. His parents were asked to appear. As soon as the boys saw that their neighbors meant business, they stopped their destructive acts. This program was so successful that the association went one step further and set up a screening committee for new tenants. Again the landlord supported them.

Asked whether the system worked, one tenant volunteered: "Certainly. When we organized and started to express our interest in how our fellow tenants behaved, the bad apples got the message. It set a new standard of behavior and the parents made their own kids behave."

The landlord or the tenants could not easily have enforced their rights in court. Criminal action against the teen-agers would only have aggravated the problem. Any attempt to collect damages from them or their parents would have been frustrating and unrewarding. Only the creation of a climate in which the tenants would restrain their own children had the possibility of success. By designing his own solution, the landlord disposed of his problem.

In many situations parties have to design their own solution because no other forum is available. In a small midwestern city a hospital and a nearby community center decided to carry out a joint $7,000,000 fund-raising drive for capital improvements. They hired a fund-raising consultant and started their drive. When the campaign ended, they were several million short. Only then did the two institutions discover that they had not decided in advance how the proceeds of the drive would be shared if they failed to reach their goal. In spite of having worked together closely in raising the funds, the groups were bitterly at odds. The chairman of the hospital board asserted that the loss should fall upon the community center because the hospital's building program was more essential to the community. He asked his lawyer to prepare a petition to the courts.

The executive director for the community center pointed out that the major part of the money had been raised from donors interested in the community center. He demanded that the money be paid over. In his turn, he threatened to sue. The joint fund-raising committee was caught in the middle.

The fund-raising consultant made a suggestion: The donors should be polled as to which organization they wanted their contribution to help. This idea was eagerly adopted. An impartial election agency was asked to mail a questionnaire to each donor and to advise the joint committee of the results. When this was done, it appeared that the executive director of the community center had been right. Over half of the money had been allocated to his organization.

A banker who served on the campaign committee explained later that the dispute could not have been resolved in any other way. "Can you imagine what would have happened to that case in court?" he asked. "Perhaps all the money would have been returned to the donors. Or the funds might have been held in escrow for years before the matter could have been solved. Now both organization will be able to carry out the major parts of their building program. It would have been tragic if these community improvements had been delayed because of the lack of a suitable decision process."

Sometimes an obligation can be enforceable, but at the same time quite illegal. A young man took over the operation of a successful restaurant when his father suddenly died. The manager told him that his father had an oral agreement to pay a retainer to a so-called "publicity agent." The title was a misnomer. The man was not expected to produce publicity. He had apparently been useful in negotiating certain arrangements with local racketeers, making it possible for the restaurant to operate without interference. Such an arrangement seemed to be necessary in that community.

The son met the "agent" and discussed the deal. "You're on the hook for a monthly payment," the man said, "and I'd prefer cash." The headwaiter of the restaurant, who had been privy to the arrangement, confirmed that the young man's father had given his word.

Here was a problem that could hardly be taken to court.

The young man was torn by indecision. He wanted to honor his father's promise, but the idea of paying for "protection" was repugnant to him. Finally he did the only thing he thought would solve his problem: He sold the business. He did not tell the purchaser about the arrangement with the publicity agent.

When the new purchaser discovered that he in turn was expected to continue to make payments to the nonproductive publicity agent, he refused. Within a week, certain incidents occurred. A rock was thrown through the front door. Garbage was dumped. The new owner changed his mind, and continued the stipend to the "publicity agent."

He threatened to sue the young man who had sold him the business. He claimed that he should have been informed about the obligation to pay the publicity agent. He had been defrauded. The young man pointed out that if a contract did exist, it was certainly an illegal contract. His problem had been solved, without benefit of a judicial remedy.

Voluntary Review Systems

Sometimes no legal remedy is available because a party's claim is based only on fairness. The other party may not be legally obligated to recognize the asserted right. When this occurs in a business connection, it is useful to seek a means of forcing a review procedure on the offending company. One such means is to organize individual parties in jeopardy and deal from a strong bargaining position. But at other times the system is offered voluntarily.

Some companies have a department of compliance to determine whether salesmen or other employees have acted in accordance with company rules and industry regulations. Customers who have a fight with a business corporation should check whether such help is available. One brokerage firm assigns its own lawyer to investigate customers' claims and to make a prompt settlement wherever the salesman is in the wrong. To avoid an investigation by the Stock Exchange, the lawyer gives the clients the benefit of every doubt.

In another company, a customer claimed that a broker had purchased two hundred shares of stock without permission. The salesman said that the customer had placed the order on the telephone. But the salesman had not bothered to obtain a confirmation of the transaction. Because of prior dealings between the salesman and the customer, the compliance attorney was personally convinced that the order had been made. But because he was unable to document it, he instructed his company to make good on the loss. He cautioned the salesman to take more care in the future and suggested that he not deal with that particular client again.

Reputable department stores, retail chains, and other concerns that deal with consumers are careful to investigate complaints that seem to have been submitted in good faith. They feel that a dissatisfied customer is a more serious liability than the loss of a questionable claim.

But the consumer should realize that records are kept on the identity of those who lodge complaints. With the widespread exchange of claims experience information, it is now relatively easy for the chronic complainer to end up on an industry blacklist. This may well prejudice his credit rating in the future and alert merchants to his cantankerous nature.

The right to review can be extremely important to the small businessman who holds a dealership from a large corporation. As long as the corporation has a unilateral right to terminate his business, he is subject to arbitrary decisions by executives of the controlling company, and is without security. Where the cancellation can be made subject to an enforceable review system, he has protection.

Some large corporations provide such systems, which can also have a useful effect upon company executives who realize that some of their decisions will be reviewed not only by their superiors, but also by an outsider.

The Carling Beer Company is a good example. Carling's president was particularly concerned that every dealer be given fair treatment, and pointed out that an impartial review system would insure compliance with the Carling policy. Like other brewing companies, Carling had experienced problems with its dealers. This problem was solved by designing an arbitration system that was entirely voluntary to the dealer. If he were terminated, he had the right to file a demand for arbitration. He could then present his case to an impartial arbitrator, a distinguished retired judge. If he won, Carling would be liable for reparation. If he lost, he could seek his remedy elsewhere.

In the absence of a union, a remedial system is sometimes provided by the corporation for its employees. The personnel department may temper each action because it can be challenged or submitted to outside scrutiny. An executive who is subject to this kind of review will think twice before he acts unfairly. One top executive requires his personnel manager to justify each dismissal as if it were being presented to an impartial arbitrator. In his organization there is a great emphasis upon "making a record." When a filing clerk was discharged recently, seventeen separate "notice of discipline" slips were found in her personnel file. She had averaged one such notice for every three months of her employment. Even in her case, the president quizzed his personnel manager, commenting that "if you had already put her on notice seventeen times, without firing her, how can you justify firing her now?" Only when the personnel manager had established the fact that the employee's performance had been even worse in recent months than in the past was the president satisfied.

An individual who is disciplined or discharged by an employer should inquire about informal as well as formal grievance procedures. In some cases, it may be well known within the organization that grievances are more likely to a fair hearing from one of the executives than from the usual personnel department functionary. But anyone who seeks to manipulate a corporate bureaucracy should pay close attention to its dynamics and not blunder into a foreseeable trap. Often the men at the top of the organization will resent any attempt to bypass executives who are more directly responsible for the problem at hand.

In one case, a vice president of a division reduced the termination pay that the personnel director of the corporation had recommended, almost as a secondary act of discipline against an employee for going directly to a top official of the company to complain about his discharge.

Voluntary review systems may not be quite as reliable, or as secure, as contractual systems based on a collective bargaining process. In the following chapter, the system of collective bargaining in labor relations, with its contractual grievance and arbitration systems, will be considered as a model for other groups, in other settings.

Chapter 7

LABOR RELATIONS
AS A MODEL

Collective bargaining of labor contracts is a good model for other kinds of group negotiations for many reasons. Enough money is involved to engage the participation of energetic and capable operators; the conflict is sufficiently interesting to capture the attention of both reporters and scholars; and other organized groups are borrowing labor techniques—strikes, picketing, boycotts, and so on—at an ever increasing rate. Collective bargaining constitutes an exciting caldron of conflict.

How does collective bargaining operate? What does it accomplish? Why does it sometimes fail?

When a union has won the right to represent a group of employees, it can require the employer to bargain over the terms of an agreement that will fix the conditions of employment for the workers it represents. Before the agreement expires, the employer is again obligated to bargain in good faith for a renewal. If the employer and the union are unable to reach a new contract by the terminal date, there may be a strike.

This section will describe some of the techniques used by both sides to settle labor disputes. Collective bargaining is interesting in itself. But more than that, it may offer hints for obtaining results in other group bargaining situations.

As one young community organizer put it: "If I could only get the people in this neighborhood [a ghetto] to act like the Teamsters, they could solve their problems in three years.

But they won't organize, they won't use their muscle, they won't stick together."

By using labor relations as a model, he hoped to accelerate improvement in his community.

Union Versus Management Rights

The Labor Management Relations Act was intended to reduce industrial strife by encouraging "employers, employees, and labor organizations" to recognize "one another's legitimate rights in their relations with each other." Section 201 of the act specifically encourages the "settlement of issues between employers and employees through the process of conference and collective bargaining between employers and the representatives of their employees." Other Federal legislation protects the union's right to bargain.

The system was not invented by Congress. A long campaign of power bargaining, persuasion, and lobbying was necessary before collective bargaining became a recognized technique.

In the beginning, no one thought it odd that armed strikebreakers were employed to terminate a strike at the iron works. A wage strike was considered an exercise in anarchy, threatening the rights of ownership. As William Miernyk points out in *Trade Unions in the Age of Affluence,* "the employers retreated from aggressive resistance, to grudging recognition, to accommodation, to acceptance and finally to cooperation." Now, many picket lines later, the strike is protected by law.

One of the great labor peacemakers, David L. Cole, describes what happened:

"There was a time when employers were free to use any of a number of strategies, for they were simply considered to be protecting their property rights in doing as they wished in operating their businesses. If the workers disliked the conditions established they could leave and work elsewhere. The courts cooperated with employers, at one time holding combinations of workers to improve their wages and other conditions to be unlawful conspiracies, and more recently disrupting the effectiveness of such organizations in injunctions and money judgments. The general opinion was that interference with the employer's freedom of action would be an impairment of his ability to operate efficiently not in keeping with the theory of free enterprise. This led to excesses because of the inequality in bargaining power, but the belief was considered warranted because of the employer's right to compete freely for the commodity called labor. Under the pressure of public opinion, corrective legislation was enacted, and before long the attitude of management itself changed. No one seriously questions any longer the propriety of such legislation, nor the right of employees to organize, nor the obligation of the employer to deal with a chosen representative as the exclusive bargaining agent for all employees in a given group. Collective bargaining is now firmly established as part of our labor policy."

As we have seen elsewhere, corporations balk at giving away their power to make unilateral decisions. This is equally true in collective bargaining. "I'll sell my business before I let the damn union tell me how to run it," not a few businessmen have uttered. And some of the bitterest contests between unions and employers have involved an issue of management rights.

For example, many companies jealously guard their right to subcontract work to outside contractors. Often their contracts with unions will prohibit this if it results in the layoff of employees who would normally perform the work. The rights under this provision often are involved in labor arbitrations. In one case a pipe company decided it would be cheaper to use outside truckers to deliver pipe. Previously, company employees had driven company trucks. One of the company drivers, transferred to a lower paid job as a result of the change, filed a grievance which was heard by an arbitrator. The company showed the arbitrator that by using outside trucking companies, it was saving money. The union contended that the important consideration was whether its members had lost jobs because of the change. The arbitrator upheld the union's position. The former truck driver was to be paid at his former rate since the contracting out had displaced him from his normal employment.

The company was outraged and wrote a letter to the arbitrator demanding that he reconsider his award: "It is decisions like yours that make employers hesitant to submit issues to outsiders. Unless the management of this company is able to decide on an economic basis whether to ship its products by company trucks or by outside carriers, we will be shackled to outmoded and inefficient methods of distribution. Your award has been a disservice to both parties."

But the union saw it differently: "Why should management be able to save money at the expense of one of our members? We're not saying that they can't ship their pipe anyway they want. All we say is that they have to pay our people a fair and reasonable wage. There is no reason why this one truck driver should subsidize the company's economy drive."

Often the issue involved in a management right controversy involves the company's ability to automate a particular process. For example, in a case filed by nine employees of a California oil-drilling company, the union claimed that the company had no right to replace machine operators when it installed automated drilling and recording equipment. This case was important because the company intended to install automatic controlled equipment at every one of its oil wells, thereby eliminating almost the entire operating force in the field. Since other jobs were not available within the company, it was necessary to let these employees go. Here, the arbitrator found that the company had the right to automate its equipment without negotiating a reduction in the work force with the union.

This time it was the union that complained to the arbitrator. A violent letter was written accusing the man of ". . . . completely disregarding the human values in the case. What may seem to you, a college professor, to be simply a question of assigning the correct meaning to a contract, is in fact a crucial turning point in the lives of these men. Consideration should have been given to the fact that they are being uprooted from their jobs and cast aside. This wealthy corporation could easily have found jobs for them elsewhere."

As the arbitrator explained to me, he really had no choice but to uphold the company. "There was no protective language in the contract. By leaving their members unprotected, the union had made it possible for the company to annihilate the bargaining unit. It was a difficult decision to make. They often are. Only disputes that can't be settled come to arbitration. Naturally, they are hard to decide."

The Application of Bargaining Power

The General Electric Corporation, with over a quarter of a million employees, is a strong negotiator. In 1947 a former marketing executive, Lemuel R. Boulware, who apparently believed that the company ought to approach labor relations as it did marketing, first articulated the G.E. philosophy of industrial relations. G.E. should find out what its employees wanted. Then it should design a compensation package that would be "right" for them.

The unions representing General Electric employees, particularly the International Union of Electrical, Radio and Machine Workers (AFL-CIO), found the Boulware approach frustrating. But for almost two decades, the company avoided crippling strikes. Whether the company's success was based upon its bargaining philosophy or upon its economic power is debatable. In 1966, on the verge of an impasse, the parties were called to Washington to reach a settlement in the shadow of the White House.

Shortly afterward, G.E. described the 1966 negotiations in detail in a pamphlet distributed to its executives. Included was a point by point description of the company's bargaining approach. The company attempted to come to the bargaining table with its "homework" thoroughly done. Prior to negotiations, it very carefully studied all of the cost factors and other considerations involved. An attempt was made to begin discussions with the union as early as possible.

Here, too, an atmosphere of educational rationalism was encouraged. The company first entered discussions with the union to exchange ideas on what settlement terms seemed indicated. Based on its own research and negotiations, the company would "attempt to put forward an offer that included everything that seemed warranted with nothing held back." (This was its avowed bargaining approach). After further negotiations, the company would only modify its offer "wherever sound reason was shown to do so," not simply in response to threats of strike or coercion.

General Electric traditionally puts great emphasis on communicating its viewpoint on bargaining issues not only to union officials, but also to employees generally and to the public.

I include G.E.'s statement of its policy because it describes what one strong company says it does in labor bargaining. Also, it summarizes the steps that would be taken in other fields if bargaining were primarily a logical process. It is not. There are many ways to reach a settlement.

For example, one well-known management representative put it this way: "We are practical men. Seeking a favorable arrangement, we consider many avenues. We are always trying to reach their people. And when we do, a satisfactory deal can usually be made." The implications of his statement ring loud and clear.

And on the union's side, great differences in the bargaining approach are also encountered. In the area of public employee unions alone, at least three quite different systems are used: the State, County, and Municipal Employees Union often negotiates by using the threat of a strike to justify wage increases; others do much of their bargaining before legislative bodies, relying upon lobbying rather than traditional collective bargaining; and the building trades union who represent public employees will base their claims on the salary level paid by private employers for similar jobs.

Whatever approach seems to insure the highest return to union members is likely to be adopted by a bargaining committee. And sometimes two or more of these techniques will be used simultaneously. Union leaders are practical men, eager to drive a hard bargain at the expense of a corporation, or, in the case of a public-employees' union, the taxpayer.

The realities of the bargaining process are as likely to be found in the economic power structure of the industry as to result from the actual bargaining. Often, by the time the bargaining session begins, both parties know the boundaries of the contract that they will have to sign. Pattern bargaining, whether by customary relationship within industry or coordinated bargaining, is on the increase. Sometimes a union will use unusually severe pressure to force employers into the national pattern. Many internationals maintain computerized records of all local agreements, and consequently are aware of how one particular contract will vary from another. Therefore local unions that have failed to achieve normal benefits may well be disposed to bring pressure upon their own bargaining committee to meet the industry standard. In these situations, the pressure can develop rapidly and quite severely.

The Teamsters achieved substantial wage gains for truck driver members during the Hoffa regime. Whether these victories were achieved because of Hoffa's bargaining skills or because of judicious use of economic force is subject to debate.

James R. Hoffa's effort was to expand control outward from his original base in Detroit, to include the entire trucking industry. To do this, Hoffa used pressure techniques suited to the long-line trucking business to apply an economic squeeze by long distance. When he wanted to extend his uniform wage structure to underpaid truckers in the southeastern states, Hoffa struck midwestern long-line carriers who operated in the Central states, until they agreed to hire Teamsters throughout their franchise territory. Then he "hostaged" these captive employers by refusing to sign with them until all southeastern carriers signed. By using a technique of "divide and conquer," he leap-frogged across the country. Strikes or the threat of strikes could force an employer to make bargaining concessions.

Bargaining is always influenced by the realities of economic power. Neither party will hesitate to apply such power. "The strike or the threat of strike is the engine that runs my union," one business agent told me. "I wouldn't get a damn thing if the boss didn't think we would hit the bricks." Having seen this man negotiate, I know that he does not hesitate to use the strike as a negotiating tool.

The Politics of Bargaining

The employers and the union prepare to bargain in different ways. Sometimes the process is simple. Management calculates how much the company can afford to pay, and reviews the increases the union has obtained from comparable companies. The union makes the same calculation, but also tries to read the temper of its membership.

"It's simple," one union leader explained, "we are selling three thousand workers. The company is buying. All we need to do is agree on the price." But it isn't that simple, by far.

The new contract is "pasted over" the prior contract. Formal bargaining is carried on in this context. Negotiation is structured upon a series of demands. Each demand is allocated a priority. To some extent the process can be visualized as a game of matching priorities. But that is to oversimplify the process.

Where do these demands come from? How are they evaluated? What are the rules under which the transaction proceeds to a conclusion?

The union is the originator of most demands, which reflect the wishes of the union constituency. In preparation, the union leaders must rationalize conflicting requirements within the bargaining unit, and discover what the members want. Sometimes this is done by open meetings of the membership.

At other times, the shop stewards of the union will visit the "grass roots" and come back with an estimate of what is needed. The union leaders then assign priorities to the demands arising from the membership.

Sometimes a great number of the members will seem preoccupied with insignificant issues. For example, in one industrial plant the condition of the washrooms became crucial in the collective bargaining. When the union leader tried to interest his members in the economic gains he was seeking for them, they would seem less interested. At the conclusion of the first bargaining meeting, the union president inspected the rest rooms. They were a shambles. When he tried to use the basins, he found that the water was turned off. Investigating further, he discovered the attendant sleeping in the service area. Apparently the attendant had discouraged use of the rest room by turning off the water during much of the day. The complaints of the workers during the collective bargaining process brought this matter to the attention of management. The attendant was promptly discharged. The rest rooms were placed in operating order. And the company promised to give closer supervision to them in the future.

In some unions the bargaining team will be made up of semiautonomous leaders who represent particular segments of the membership. The chief union negotiator will then be speaking for a restless coalition of voices rather than a monolithic organization.

Leadership may form around a faction in the membership. In one large industrial company, the working force had been built up during periods of capital expansion. There was an older group of workers in their forties and fifties. There were a growing number of younger people. The union leaders, drawn from the older segment of the membership, found it difficult to hold the loyalty of the younger employees.

Young and aggressive business agents were able to acquire an identifiable constituency and to exercise independent power in dealing with the union leadership. In collective bargaining, they were able to make their own demands, which they forced the leadership to recognize. These demands were presented during collective bargaining and won as prizes for their voters. The chief negotiator for the union had to respond to the demands of these new leaders. He had to obtain something for each of them during the negotiations and be sure that the final package contained enough improvements to gain their approval.

In one New York union, changes in the composition of the membership had produced factions of ethnic minority groups. The president, an Irishman who had been on the job for many years, found himself increasingly circumscribed by the growing power of his vice presidents who represented their own nationalities. He knew that in a few years their combined votes would displace him as head of the union. His best hope to maintain office would be to obtain the support by promising them portions of their collective bargaining package for their own ethnic constituency. For several two-year contracts, this leader succeeded, at the price of compromising the wishes and demands of his own constituency. Finally, two vice presidents combined their strength, mounted an insurgent campaign against him, and in a hotly contested election, removed him.

There is a constant interplay and competition between union leaders, each seeking to satisfy his own supporters, each jockeying for position to obtain more benefits from the collective bargaining process and to retain his own position in the union hierarchy. Individual power within the union is a transient thing. Union leaders must learn to accommodate to the incoherent but inconsistent desires of the membership.

"I am tired of politics," one union president told me when I asked him why he was hunting a job. "As a union leader, I am always under the gun. I am campaigning for election every day of the year. If one of my members sees me sitting in a bar, they think I'm goofing off. This is too political a job. I want to lead my own life."

Sometimes such a leader is tempted to resolve his problems by reaching a secret agreement with management. This can be hazardous because a prearrangement is difficult to conceal. Where such a deal becomes known, the leader is subject to attack by the factional voices that sit beside him at the table. Union leaders have been deposed because the rank and file decided that they were too close to management and no longer accurately reflected the real wishes of the workers.

David McDonald, former president of the Steelworkers, is a case in point. His friendship with top steel executives, his home in Palm Springs, and his lavish way of life, may have contributed to his rejection by the voters. In addition, McDonald had attempted to disengage some of the mutual problems of management and labor in the steel industry from the traditional collective bargaining process, to be discussed and resolved in study committees during the term of the contract. This was presented by his opponents as an attempt to handle labor management bargaining in an undemocratic way, with arrangements made privately, outside the scrutiny of the general membership and its duly elected representatives. In this atmosphere, it was possible for McDonald's opponents to imply that he was making secret agreements with management and no longer represented the militant demands of his union members.

Labor Negotiation—Preparing and Processing

A recent advertisement for a labor service asked: "What is the big problem in labor relations?" and answered: "Getting the right facts—fast!"

Both sides must gather relevant information. What are the right facts? Again, negotiators must know how much the company can afford to pay, what potential labor savings are available, what the union has been getting elsewhere. Current union agreements with comparable companies must be reviewed, and economic data must be collected. The company must obtain operating information from line supervision. Comprehensive preparation and coordination of the bargaining effort is necessary. Only then can the company's bargaining position and tactics be formulated.

"What is the most important part of collective bargaining?"
I asked a top negotiator in the steel industry.

"Doing my homework. Knowing in advance where we are
likely to come out. Understanding how we are going to get
there."

"How about your skills as a negotiator?"

"Ninety percent of the job is preparation. The worst
negotiators are the heroes who try to come in during the tenth
inning and make a deal on the basis of their genius for bargaining. This is a profession, not an exercise in creative writing."

The most important decision for the employer is to select
the chief negotiator. This may precipitate a power struggle
within the hierarchy of the company over who will call the
shots. Usually he will be a man who has access to top executives.
Although the chief negotiator has the help of a bargaining
team, he usually has a strong voice in making decisions, in most
cases, even an arbitrary voice. His selection is of extreme importance.

. The structure of the union may influence this decision.
Management will try to select a man who can obtain the best
possible deal from the union. This is generally a man who has
prestige in the eyes of the union representatives. His style
should be compatible with that of the union leadership. Labor
negotiations are too important to risk their being disrupted
by a personality clash between negotiators. Sometimes the
union will try to wrangle the replacement of a tough bargainer.
But management will seldom knowingly permit the union to
participate in the selection process.

The negotiator will have to establish a personal relationship with the union, at least until the long negotiation is concluded. This intimate but hostile partnership creates its own
ethical code. A temporary gain may sometimes be made through
deception or distortion of facts. But usually a lie will be discovered. The negotiator's credibility is imputed to the party he
represents. In long-range relationships, any attempt to profit
by unethical conduct will reduce the negotiator's credibility in
the future. Where a lie is disclosed, the other party is likely
to make the controversy a matter of principle, refusing to settle
until forced to do so.

In a recent labor negotiation in the South, an inexperienced industrial relations director was able to persuade a union to take a cent or two less than they were demanding, on the basis of comparative wage figures that he said he had obtained from other employers in the area. After the contract was signed, the union president checked the figures with the companies named. He was bitterly angry to discover that the figures were inaccurate. In fact, these companies had no recollection of having discussed their wages with the company man. They did not even know him.

The union president went to the industrial relations director and told him to his face that he was a liar. Then he reported him to the company president. The man was replaced.

"We do not want this man representing us in labor contract negotiations," the president said. "His word is our word. Unless the union believes what we say, a sound relationship is impossible."

The management negotiator must be completely familiar with the company and its production facilities. He should be intimately acquainted with the collective bargaining contract and how it developed. He must have a working knowledge of labor relations and be conversant with the legal structure under which it is carried out. Once selected, his full time should be available. He will find it difficult to schedule any other work during the critical negotiating period, and must guard himself from interruptions. Sessions scheduled for an afternoon have a way of extending themselves into the evening, through the night and next morning. Sometimes emergencies explode. He may have to schedule secret meetings or shuttle between formal negotiations and the courts.

Each negotiation is different. Some are peculiarly important because they involve large numbers of employees and relatively novel bargaining situations. Others involve only a few workers and have minor importance.

In the negotiation of a labor contract for a small auto repair shop, the general manager of the shop carried out the entire bargaining process himself. The terms and conditions of "pattern contracts" that had been negotiated for similar shops in the city were binding on his shop. His function was to follow the leader, agreeing to the gains the union had not yet won in other shops. (The owner of the business, a leading industrialist from another state, did not authorize his manager to hire a labor relations expert to assist with the bargaining.)

In the negotiations of a large, multiplant employer, the bargaining was done by a team of fifteen men, two of whom were outside attorneys. The team was led by the vice president for industrial relations.

After the union's demands were "on the table," the company responded. The company spokesman ostentatiously ignored the "impractical" demands and discussed the others. The company sometimes presented its own demands, usually to clarify contract language or to re-establish some principle that had eroded by past practice or by an arbitration award.

In responding to those demands that it felt were presented seriously, the corporation would sometimes "price out" an improvement in wages or fringe benefits. This involved complicated exhibits and factual presentations. From time to time, facts were challenged by the union. Rational presentations were often punctuated, sometimes for political reasons, by violent attacks upon the other side or upon individuals.

There is "accountability" in collective bargaining. Union leaders bring pressure to bear on any executive they believe has been unfair in his treatment of union members during the previous contract period. I remember one bargaining agent who presented a convincing case against the director of the health department of a corporation. Lazy administration, sloppy handling of case records, and mistreatment of individual workers were described in great detail. When the whole case had been presented against this executive, it was clear that the company would not defend him. The management negotiator asked for time to look into the practices of that department. At the next bargaining session, the company announced that the health director had been replaced by another executive.

Occasionally an attack will be directed against operating managers. A production manager in a furniture factory had made arbitrary decisions about assignments, which had created many grievances. At the contract negotiations that year, the union took one full day to present its case against the manager. The company negotiator acknowledged that he was a problem. Family problems had put him under too much pressure. He was transferred to a less demanding job until he recovered. To this extent, collective bargaining can have a healthy impact upon the working conditions within the bargaining unit.

Sometimes a benign union leader may permit aggressive lieutenants to attack the company, asking for far more than the union expects to get. The union president may then urge that he alone stands between the company and a mob of militant leaders. Conversely, the leader himself may take the role of the difficult-to-deal-with negotiator. After the formal negotiating session, other members of the union bargaining team may offer to restrain their leader if the company is willing to make more concessions.

The management team can sometimes use this strategy. But management usually desires to present a monolithic position. In multiemployer bargaining, alleged differences of opinion can be used by the chief negotiator to suggest that he is attempting to protect the union against the inordinate demands of one or more of his colleagues.

Sometimes such a role is unintentional, and represents the expression of the personalities of those on one side of the table. Labor bargaining is an art partially because one never knows whether a particular characterization by a negotiator is "for real." There is an element of bluff at all times. Every display of emotion is carefully analyzed by the other side to determine what it means and what it is intended to mean.

The basic transaction is to sell the other side into making concessions. What will the traffic bear? What will happen if an agreement is not reached? Promises, threats, logic, and other tools are used to persuade the other side to move toward a compromise.

Since a great deal of money is involved, nerves are taut. The tension affects negotiators in different ways. Some become taciturn. Others become garrulous, making boring statements and restatements about their organization's position. The pressure to understand and appraise the opponent's position and the long hours increase the tension. One company and union require continuous negotiations with only brief recesses for eating and sleeping. No one can leave the hotel. There is no contact with outsiders. The company and the union guarantee that their negotiators abide by these rules. The intention is to increase the pressure on both sides to settle their differences.

One negotiator who has gone through several of these

sessions told me that it works. "You have to experience it to believe it. After two or three days in that hotel, I'd sell my wife into a salt pit for thirty-seven cents. It's like being in prison. But it results in settlements. We think the rules are justified."

Particular companies and unions develop a traditional, predictable behavior at the bargaining table. In some cases an almost benedictory shower of insults from the union's side will fall upon the company team at the very beginning of the sessions. In other cases, it will be traditional for the union leader to get up and leave the room in what appears to be a rage. At other times the company negotiator will play some traditional role in the proceedings.

When leadership changes, one sometimes sees an attempt by the new team to change the format of the proceedings. Then the other side must decide whether the format is being changed for change's sake or whether a meaningful amendment in the agenda has taken place.

The formal meetings are not the only activities during the days of negotiation. Even more useful meetings may take place between representatives of the company and the union, during which particular wage and benefit areas can be frankly discussed. But, in addition, bargainers are constantly probing the decision-making power of the other side. Management may suspect that the nominal head of the union cannot make unilateral decisions, that he is only a façade behind which shifting power alliances are resolved. During one bargaining session, the following exchange took place.

The company negotiator, speaking to the union president, said: "We have priced out your pension demands and might be inclined to make them part of the settlement package. But since only 15 percent of your members are within ten years of retirement age, we thought that you might need some time to see whether this is acceptable to your people."

The union president replied: "We will be having a caucus at lunch, and I can give you our position on that this afternoon." (By indicating his need to confer with his team on this question, the leader disclosed that the "youth faction" was represented on this bargaining team.) And there is a sophisticated sense of timing. The spokesmen must understand exactly when a new argument should be thrown upon the table and what reaction should be made in response to a move by the other side. By interjecting himself decisively at the appropriate time, he may be able to turn one group against the other to his own benefit.

A manufacturer had encountered difficulty in promoting younger workers because of an inflexible seniority system. He was trying to obtain a relaxation of this procedure by citing examples of younger men who had been deprived of better jobs because they were not next in line in the seniority ladder. The union president, an older man, was smart enough to see what the company was attempting. When the company personnel director had described the third example the union leader winked at him and said, "We are getting the message, George. We realize that the young people in this bargaining unit are increasing. Let me have your case stories of young kids being blocked by the seniority system. We could read them at a union meeting—I am kidding, of course." In the final settlement, the union agreed to be more flexible about seniority.

In every negotiation there comes a time when the piecemeal discussions must be resolved into a bargain. Sometimes this point is reached rapidly. At other times, it is necessary for the negotiator to wait patiently until the logical time for finalization. Patience is a quality that should be encouraged in every negotiator. The experienced operator will sit through interminable discussions, probing, responding, and waiting for the appropriate time to exercise initiative.

One advantage of extended negotiations is that it is possible to advance the parties gradually toward each other, giving the union constituency the impression that progress is being made. Every concession by the company reduces the likelihood of a strike. Thus, the company is able to melt away the idea that a work stoppage will be needed to break an impasse. Union leaders need an emotional issue if they are to persuade themselves and their membership that a strike is necessary. The management negotiator should diligently avoid giving the union such an issue.

A small company and union were negotiating the first renewal of their collective bargaining contract. The plant manager dominated the meeting. He told the union that he and his personnel director had carefully studied the contract. He had also reviewed the company's finances with the comptroller. As he saw it, there were only three areas in which the company could make concessions. An overall wage increase could be made. Two new holidays could be added. And the company would be willing to pay a larger share of medical insurance. As far as he could see, the size of the wage increase was the only bargainable issue. He asked the union to go ahead on that basis.

They looked at him in astonishment. They had expected to take up most of the first meeting in simply reporting their many demands to management. It was impossible for them to abandon their plan. The members would have accused the bargaining committee of a sellout.

An old shop steward, sitting at the end of the table, leaned over and said: "That fool is asking us to cut our throats before we even sit down at the table."

But the union president had already launched a furious tirade against the plant manager, claiming that he was refusing to bargain, was being insolent to the workers, and did not deserve anything more than a strike. He finally calmed down and agreed to have one of his assistants read through a long list of union demands. But when he left the room he was still muttering to himself about the stupidity of the management negotiator.

Why had the plant manager opened the negotiations in such an unconventional way? "Well," he said, "I just thought I could save all of us a good deal of time. I had a hunch that I knew where we would end up on this deal. It seemed like the fastest way to reach an agreement."

"What do you think now?" he was asked.

"Maybe I made a mistake. They seem awfully mad about something. Maybe next time I better just sit and listen."

The negotiations then took on a much more traditional format. When the contract was signed, after five more bargaining sessions, the plant manager was acting like a professional.

The union president had warmed up enough to kid the manager: "We were shocked when you unloaded your bag of rocks at the first session. After that, most of my people thought we were going to have a strike. Don't ever do that to us again. If our members didn't think we bargained hard and long, you'd see a new set of faces across the table. Don't make our job any harder than it is."

Will Union Membership Accept the Agreement?

After the union negotiator has assembled the desires of union members into a package of demands which he then has to sell to the employer, he is faced with still another transaction.

Following an agreement with the employer, the union negotiator must explain the contract to his members, showing why he and his committee conceded on certain demands, and compromised others.

This is a harsh test of his leadership and ability. More than one union leader has been insulted and booed at the ratification meeting, and escorted from the hall by a protective police cordon.

At a meeting in Manhattan Center in New York City, the membership of one local virtually erupted, throwing chairs and bottles until the union officers scrambled to safety behind the stage.

How can the union leadership protect itself against such a situation? First, the leaders should be reasonably sure that the improvements in the new contract are well understood by the membership and are satisfactory in amount. Preliminary meetings should be held with shop stewards to determine whether there is general satisfaction with the results of the negotiations.

If the shop stewards report an organized effort to reject the contract, there are some practical ways to avoid a chaotic rejection meeting. The ratification vote can be made by mail or through the use of voting machines. If it is necessary to hold an open meeting, great care can be taken as to the physical facilities, the time of day set for the meeting, and the chairman's ability to run the meeting skillfully. The location of microphones, the access to the dais area, and the checking of credentials of those who will be permitted to enter the hall can be extremely important to the decorum of the meeting. A planning meeting should certainly be held by the union leadership to decide how to present the contract in a way that will make it most likely to be accepted.

One union always tries to schedule membership meetings at a time and location that are most favorable for the employees who are most likely to support the incumbent officers. In this union, many youthful workers on the night shift find it difficult to attend meetings. This is done by design.

Of course, a different set of considerations faces those members of the union who wish to reject a contract. A faction that decides to work for rejection will have to engage in an organizing effort to persuade individual members to vote against the contract. Tactical decisions will have to be made, with an organized plan in mind. This may involve the disruption of a membership meeting. At other times, it may involve a telephone campaign, a mailing to the membership, informational pickets, or some other method to bring the facts to the attention of the individual union members so that they will be motivated to vote against the contract.

The approval of a collective bargaining contract by the membership is a referendum. All of the democratic techniques that are useful in connection with other elections are also applicable in this situation.

One additional option of the union officers may be to "buy off" the leaders of the rejection movement. Such a tactic must be entered into with great care, since an unsuccessful offer can be publicized by the insurgents to gain additional support for rejecting the contract.

Beyond these tactical considerations, it should be recognized that some contracts are simply not good enough. There, the rejection vote will simply show that the membership is not satisfied with the bargaining results of its leadership. Even the most astute preplanning will probably not guard against a strong ground swell of rejection. In such a case, the leadership may be well advised to arrange that the rejection vote be taken with as little fanfare as possible and to return to the bargaining table in an attempt to force further concessions from the employer.

An increasing number of contracts are being rejected in ratification votes. One well-publicized example is the rejection by the International Machinists of a contract obtained from six national airlines. In the New York City garbage strike, the president of the union, John DeLury, after accepting what seemed to be a generous offer from the city, appeared before a large number of union members intending to recommend that a contract be signed. Before he could explain why he believed the offer was a good one, his membership nearly mobbed him, demanding a city-wide strike to force the mayor to increase his offer. Apparently afraid to stand up against the demands of the union members, DeLury led his men into an unpopular garbage strike that created mounds of rotted debris throughout the city streets.

Secretary of Labor W. Willard Wirtz has warned that membership rejections of negotiated contracts can be "very, very dangerous for collective bargaining" because they might become a deliberate technique for escalating the ultimate settlement. Nevertheless, the membership's right to reject an agreement is part of the price that must be paid for strengthening the voice of the individual union member.

The Labor Grievance Procedure

One of the important dispute settlement techniques devised in labor management is the contractual grievance procedure. A union member can ask his union to file a grievance for him if he thinks that the company has violated his rights under the collective bargaining agreement. The procedure is always spelled out in the labor contract.

The first step may be for the shop steward to bring the grievance to the attention of a foreman. If no settlement is reached, an official of the union may present it to the personnel department. Finally, if the parties cannot dispose of the dispute by agreement, the union usually has a right to demand arbitration.

A typical case: An employee in a plastic products factory had been employed for almost five years. His new job involved mixing batches of chemicals. Although he had been trained for a month and had shown an ability to perform this function, he made a series of blunders. His latest mistake had been particularly dangerous—one of the ingredients could have caused an explosion. He was demoted.

The union claimed that the employer did not have the right to demote a man once he had qualified for the job. The company argued that the job was too critical; nor were they willing to pay the higher rate.

Since neither the union nor the employer would back down, this case had to be arbitrated. After listening to the testimony submitted by both sides, the arbitrator agreed with the employer, ruling that although the employee had completed the training program and had been appointed to the job, the company had a right to demote him. His demotion for incompetence was not a form of discipline. Management had a duty to see that employees in dangerous assignments were well trained and competent. Therefore, the arbitrator said, "Demotion in this type of case was not disciplinary demotion. It was a tool for matching the man to the job."

The international representative who tried this case for the union was not unduly distressed by the arbitrator's award. As he put it, "This damn fool would have blown the plant sky high if he hadn't been taken off the job. I had to process his grievance because the boys felt that the company ought to be taught a lesson for selecting such a stupid jerk for promotion into a dangerous job. When I suggested that we couldn't win the case, they told me to file it anyway, if only to make the company admit how foolish it had been in the first place. I didn't press the issue too hard. I guess the arbitrator read my signals."

A fair number of labor arbitrations are filed because the rank and file of the union want them for political purposes, even though the leadership has every expectation of losing them.

Individual members of the union can manipulate the grievance procedure to improve the conditions of their own particular jobs. The union member should be familiar with the organizational structure of the union. He has to be sure that the shop steward or the union business manager will listen to his request sympathetically. The more political power the member controls within the bargaining unit, the more likely that the union officials will take him seriously. A group of employees are more apt to be served than a single union member, so that organizing skills can sometimes be important in bringing on a grievance.

An individual member who wants to improve his job conditions through the grievance procedure should first recruit other employees who have a common interest, often holding a planning meeting, and then should present the case to the union for action. If the union is sympathetic, officials can be drawn into the planning so that a maximum impact is made upon the employer. Most disputes are resolved in the early stages of the grievance procedure and do not have to go to arbitration. But sometimes the company will not give in. Then an arbitration will have to be filed. If enough popular support has been obtained for the grievance, the union leadership will be forced to take it to an arbitrator.

Political considerations are often obvious in the grievance and arbitration process. An insurgent leader can make a name for himself by forcing the union to process a case to arbitration and then winning the case. Because arbitration frequently provides a dramatic confrontation between the grievant and the company, it may offer high visibility for the union official responsible for moving the case.

For example, a union shop steward was fired by his employer for stealing a typewriter from the company personnel department. A full-scale arbitration hearing was carried out between the union and the company. The company produced three witnesses who testified that they saw the shop steward carry the typewriter out of the office, put it in his car, and drive away. The arbitrator asked the union attorney, "Why is this case in arbitration?"

"I object to your question," the union lawyer snapped. "It is not your concern why the union is contesting this discharge. That's our problem. Your job is to decide whether this man was fired for cause."

The arbitrator did not press the attorney. After he rendered an award in favor of the company, he learned why it had been necessary for the union to process the case.

The shop steward had been a popular political leader within the union. At one of the membership meetings, a friend of his had claimed that the steward was being railroaded by other union leaders.

"The leadership doesn't dare bring this out into the open," he charged. "I say the man deserves a chance to be heard."

Popular support for this view forced the union leadership to decide that even though the company's charges appeared to be true, the case had to be arbitrated.

But most labor arbitration cases involve genuine differences of opinion between the parties. Many of them involve questions of whether or not dismissal or discipline by the employer was for just cause.

For example, one recent case involved a discharge of an employee who admitted that he had "fifteen to twenty beers" before reporting to work, but who nevertheless managed to perform his "material handling" duties until he became ill and was escorted out of the plant.

The labor contract between the parties permitted "discharge without warning" for drunkenness. But nevertheless an arbitrator found that the evidence fell far short of establishing a condition of major drunkenness. The arbitrator was influenced by the fact that the grievant exhibited no belligerency as he was escorted from the plant, he created no disturbance, and the supervisor did not remove him from his work until he became ill. Furthermore the foreman on the job did not think it necessary to deter the grievant from driving thirteen miles to his home. Therefore the company was ordered to put the grievant back on the payroll.

Sometimes the union will refuse to file a grievance. An individual employee-grievant does not have to passively acquiesce. He should find within the union an appropriate champion. Since the union has discretion as to how much it will fight the company to save a member's job, it is in the employer's interest to be sure that his case is given a high priority. His problem is how to persuade the officers of the union to press his case. Can he create a lobby? Do the facts show that he was unfairly treated? Can a victory in his case be useful to a shop steward who takes up the cudgels on his behalf? These questions show how a grievance may be intimately connected with the internal reward system of the union itself. The first consideration of the union member should be to study the personalities and interests of the union leaders, to determine whom he will have to convince as to the priority of his case.

Arbitration cases seem relatively insignificant in the reading. But they involve industrial relations issues which are important to the employees involved. The genius of the labor arbitration system is that such controversies can be decided promptly and intelligently without disturbing the ongoing relationship between the union and the employer.

Admittedly, in more substantial cases, such as those involving large numbers of employees, both parties are likely to turn the labor arbitration into a formal adversary procedure, with attorneys representing both sides and with meticulous preparation and presentation of the issues.

For example, a recent grievance between a United Automobile Workers local and a foundry, on behalf of all employees having seniority of at least one year, in which the union requested accrued vacation pay, would undoubtedly involve a large number of employees, a substantial amount of money, and a strong effort by both parties.

Small inconsequential cases are accorded summary treatment, while larger and more significant cases receive an almost unlimited amount of time and attention. Being contractual, the labor arbitration system can be flexible and appropriate for the particular case involved.

Can Collective Bargaining and Grievance Arbitration Resolve Other Kinds of Disputes?

If collective bargaining seems to provide a reasonable solution for the fixing of wages, might not the same technique be useful in other areas of dispute between organized individuals and institutions? There are many settings in which a similar arrangement might take root.

Marketing negotiations between farmers and purchasers of their crops, rents and standards of building maintenance between tenants and landlords, contractual arrangements between franchise holders and franchise corporations, and disputes between parents and educational institutions are only a few examples. Of course, wages and working conditions of presently unorganized workers and employers; students and schools; prisoners and prisons; welfare claimants and public agencies. All these settings are in the process of change. Where it was once unthinkable for the weak and unorganized to challenge the hierarchy of an entrenched institution, the student strike and the prison riot have become fashionable. A group at Cornell University published a report entitled *The Ineffective Soldier*. That study reviewed hundreds of appeals filed by soldiers who had been disciplined by the army during World War II. In some cases, the penalty was mitigated because of considerations of mental incapacity, physical exhaustion, or emotional disturbance. Even during a national crisis, democratic values could be injected into the relationship of soldier and state.

In many such situations, the collective bargaining system for resolving disputes between groups of individuals and institutions would seem to have good potential. This should be of interest to anyone who finds himself in an adverse position with a corporation, a government agency, or some other institution, where alone he is powerless and unprotected, but working in concert with his fellows he may be able to mount a joint campaign against a common adversary.

The institutions themselves may be increasingly eager to consent to the installation of an impartial grievance system, if for no better reason than that if they do not it is likely that government intervention will take place. Increasingly, government agencies are being urged to give representation and organized power to various groups of disadvantaged individuals. So the clock may be running against the possibility of devising voluntary systems.

In other countries, it is almost unthinkable that individual grievances will not be settled through some form of government regulation. For example, in South America almost every dispute between workers and employers is submitted to a government agency for a decision.

Chapter 8

ORGANIZING TO BRING ABOUT CHANGE

This chapter will discuss the creation and control of group power, often the key to success in waging an adversary campaign. Since the days of the tomahawk and the frontier blockhouse, our society has emphasized voluntary action by private groups. Organization provides the power to impose group desires upon a seemingly overwhelming and impersonal culture. To the impatient individual who wants to win his battle, it is often far better to operate through an organization than to try to file a lawsuit or to process a grievance through traditional administrative channels. The possibility of organizing a pressure group or using the power of an existing organization should always be considered in appropriate cases.

A lady who has led several successful crusades to reform the operation of city agencies in Boston puts it this way: "Whenever my group receives a complaint about still another bureaucratic stupidity, we set up a task force to devise a battle plan. First we marshal our allies. What organizations are likely to take up the fight against this particular nonsense? How much are they likely to contribute to an action fund? Then we recruit a small committee to take personal responsibility for mounting the attack. Who had standing with the particular agency? Who can we get to commit their time? Who will give the matter first priority? Where can we borrow some workers? Only when we have our own forces organized, do we start planning our attack."

The intelligent and effective approach of this successful

community leader should be emulated by anyone who wants to create change or to contest against corporations, government agencies, or other institutions.

In discussing group conflict, we must consider a wide variety of settings. A few situations capture the attention of the wider public and are well known. Thousands of others do not. The controversy may be local. A contested school bond referendum may seem important to the residents of a suburb, but may not even be mentioned in the metropolitan press. Sometimes the dispute will arise among a specialized group. The general public may have no interest in the issue. Nevertheless such disputes are important to the participants, and to others affected by them.

The general techniques of such group manipulations are similar even in many different settings—the creation of Black Power groups may be accomplished by the same methods used to take over the State Dental Association.

Politicians and others who manipulate power are increasingly aware of the need to harness organizations and groups. A state senator who is a frequent target for lobbyists explained it this way, "Very little of significance happens today through the efforts of an individual. Group power is what changes things. When somebody asks for my help, I am interested in how many votes he can sway. Where is his public support? How influential is the group for whom he speaks?" "Power politics" is not an idle phrase. It is the very essence of dispute settlement where disputes concern the public interest.

How to Build Your Own Organization

How can you create an organization for your own ends? It may be as simple as forming an *ad hoc* pressure group to achieve a limited goal.

For example, in my neighborhood in New York City, three mothers decided that the equipment in the playground was inadequate for their children. Meetings were held. Resolutions were passed. Then these mothers marching under a barrage of letters obtained from their husbands trooped into the mayor's office. They did not see him. But they saw his assistant, who assured them that the mayor understood their problem, and that the Parks Department, responsible for the equipment, would be told to cooperate. The momentum of their campaign generated donations of private funds. The mothers solicited funds in their apartment houses. A benefit dance was held, with the proceeds going to the renovation of the playground. A foundation made a matching grant.

Soon after, the playground was surveyed. Ground was broken. Concrete turtles and other climbable objects appeared. Safety surfacing was spread under the swings and slides. Within a few months, a substantial improvement had been made. This was accomplished in a city where the Parks Department budget is notoriously meager.

Operating informally may be effective where activities are directed toward a crisis situation or on a sporadic basis. But when an organization must be created for a continuing campaign, formal structure is advisable. An organizational meeting should be held at the very beginning of the campaign. Bylaws should be prepared, preferably by a lawyer. The aims and objectives of the organization should be agreed upon. Officers should be elected and action committees appointed. The structure of the organization should be carefully designed to carry out the program in which the members are interested. Most organizations will need some working committees: an executive committee to direct policy; a committee responsible for obtaining adequate financial support; a nominating committee so that additions to the board of directors can be carefully selected; and one or more program committees to direct the activities.

Very often, the founders of the organization will not be able to give their full time to the organization. Where possible, a staff should be hired to do the day-to-day work. But, unless full time workers are available, it is unlikely that an effective job will be done. In order to hire effective staff, it is necessary to obtain enough funds to pay them and to provide the space, equipment, and expenses which they will need to operate.

Where would unions be were they not able to produce operating revenue through membership dues? Other organizations must find similar sources of income to meet necessary costs too. Often the failure to obtain adequate financial support weakens an agency to the point where it can no longer cope with the tasks it has set itself.

One citizens' organization dedicated to reforming the political climate of a large city became increasingly ineffectual because its original founders lost their ability to raise the money needed to carry out research and public relations that were required to inform the public of graft and corruption within the city administration. The part-time, voluntary research of the organization did not penetrate far enough beneath the surface. The organization's publicity did not reach enough people to make an appreciable impact. This organization starved itself to death because it was unable to raise operating funds.

How will your organization finance itself? A thorough study must be made of the fund-raising potential of the particular organization in light of the kinds of jobs that it wants to do. Particularly where the organization will be entering an important conflict, its supporters should plan its financial requirement in advance.

The wisdom of foresight can be seen in an example of one organization that had always been able to raise funds for settlement work in a slum neighborhood. It soon found that much of its support evaporated when it sponsored a rent strike. Eventually, the board of directors fired the agency's militant director and involved the agency in less controversial activities.

If fund-raising is going to be required, the organization should seek professional advice to determine what kinds of people or what organizations are likely to volunteer support. Then a program should be designed for soliciting these target areas. A fund drive for a civil rights organization must be done in quite a different way from a solicitation for funds to defeat a civilian review board. Who will support the aims of the organization? Where may funds be raised most effectively and economically? What techniques should be used? The organization must compete for money, public attention, volunteer workers, and all other support. The competition between social agencies for operating funds is harsh and unremitting. Each organization must identify its program in the public mind and establish its needs. Newspaper articles must be placed and the attention of television and radio must be captured. Effective manipulation of publicity is the organizer's artillery. Professional skill is often needed. The amateur may fail to place his message in the appropriate media. Communication may become garbled, lose its impact, or fail to reach the attention of the appropriate public.

Entree to the media, skill in designing the information package, and appropriate timing and insight into the "newsability" of the item are important working talents of a public relations specialist. These skills are vital because the program of the organization must be carried out in a public context.

Both the staff and the volunteers will have to be committed to the tasks ahead. As an organizer, this will be one of your most difficult jobs.

You must create enthusiasm for the campaign ahead, at least until you have built an adequate organization for carrying out the work. Even then, the dedication of board members and other supporters must be renewed constantly, to insure that an optimum effort is being made by each of them. The organization should carefully cultivate every possible source of help so that its full potential can be brought to bear upon a dispute.

A committee was formed in one midwestern city to stamp out the sale of pornographic books at magazine stores. Several thousand dollars were raised from the community. Lawsuits were initiated to prohibit the sale of such literature. Talks were given at local service clubs. Many groups made platforms available for the committee.

But after a few months of activity, work came to a halt. For one thing, it became difficult to raise funds to pay legal fees. A lawyer who had been elected vice president of the committee handled some of the cases without compensation, but he had a fight with the president. She had accused him of not being aggressive enough in processing the cases entrusted to him. He told her that he "would be damned if he'd handle her cases at the expense of his law practice." The owner of a magazine store filed a lawsuit against every member of the committee, alleging that they had unlawfully interfered with his business. The lawsuit persuaded several members to resign. Obviously the organizers were unable to maintain the enthusiasm of their supporters.

As the vice-chairman put it, "Why should we expose ourselves to harassment? What are the other parents doing? If they would keep this smut out of the hands of their children, there would be no problem."

The magazine-store operator withdrew his lawsuit upon the understanding that the committee would go out of business. On this basis, a settlement was arranged.

How to Create a Bargaining Relationship

Another aspect of how you can use a new organization is the problem of creating a bargaining relationship with your adversary. Why should your opponent bargain with you or with your new organization? What gives you a right to demand a confrontation?

Particularly where your organization intends to represent the interests of other individuals, you and your associates will have to establish your right to speak, to demand, and to lay claim to a contractual relationship with the other party. Much of the seeming disorder, violence, and social breakdown which is so repetitively reported by our news media, stems from this need to establish bargaining relationships on behalf of incoherent and disorganized groups of individuals. The process may easily be understood by looking at how groups have won their fights for exclusive representation, as we have done in the last chapter where we saw unions bargain for all employees against the employer. The lesson learned there is the importance of obtaining an exclusive collective bargaining relationship. We have seen that in the field of labor relations this right was first gained by collective power, and confirmed by law.

Outside labor, such a relationship may be created in a variety of ways, most of which involve bringing economic pressure to bear upon the institution or organization involved.

Your new organization will have to show the opposing institution that it must negotiate in self-interest, that there is no other alternative.

Consider the organizing efforts now being carried out by the tenants of apartment projects, in both private and public housing. Why should a landlord ever agree to bargain with representatives of his tenants? The tenants are interested in such a relationship because they want to improve the building maintenance, eliminate bad social conditions, and perhaps even reduce the rents. They have a natural interest in reducing the cost and improving the quality of their housing. But why should the landlord waive his right to deal with each tenant individually, capitalizing on their lack of organization by charging whatever rent the traffic will bear and by providing a bare minimum of building service?

In situations where tenant organizations have been successful in establishing an exclusive bargaining relationship with a landlord, they have used a battery of pressure techniques. Often, the landlord had been pressured into a negotiation by a rent strike. His fixed operating costs on the property often make him particularly sensitive to any threat of delayed rental payments. This weapon is often the first and most effective step in the union's bargaining activities.

In the meantime, pressure can also be generated with municipal agencies and through the press. High-visibility picketing at sensitive points of the landlord's organization can escalate the pressure. Picketing by tenants of apartment projects is now a common sight in urban centers. Well-publicized meetings, task forces of union organizers, and all of the apparatus of serious group pressure are often encountered in these situations.

The representative of a successful tenant union in Chicago told a legislative subcommittee how important recognition was for the tenant union: "Tenant unions today, in the city of Chicago, are in the process of fighting to achieve recognition and to be allowed to voice their ideas regarding the problems of slum housing. But as the history of the labor movement shows us, this recognition will never come about automatically; unions must be given the tools to force recognition. The rent strike is solely for the purpose of achieving recognition for the union and of forcing the landlord to sit down and negotiate a collective bargaining agreement covering the conditions under which people can live in decent housing."

But as well as the "stick" of the rent strike and the picket, the tenant organization can offer the landlord the "carrot" of tenant stability and self-regulation. Members of the tenant union have a personal interest in excluding "bad neighbors." The union can agree to screen incoming tenants, to discipline tenants who do not abide by customary behavior, and to refuse to process the grievance of tenants who make unjustified demands upon the landlord.

Whether the landlord welcomes the participation of the tenant union, or accepts it only because he must for economic reasons, it is essential to the union that an exclusive bargaining relationship be created.

A professor at a school of social work, who has served as a consultant to organizations in a Negro ghetto, is discouraged about his constituency engaging in effective bargaining: "My people negotiate with their hearts, not with their minds. Disorganized, demoralized, and profoundly inept, their efforts are less effective than the school debating society. They have no power, no plan, and damn little leadership. Sometimes, I am ready to throw in the towel."

He asked where such a group could get training in the skills of negotiations. Labor unions have been suggested as a source of help. But he wonders whether his clients could work with union organizers. Will traditional labor bargaining techniques work where the group desires are so incoherent and where the right to represent is so tenuous?

"I doubt it," he said. "My people are only able to respond to crisis."

Sometimes a group will lack the most basic skills. This was true in one housing project, operated by the Housing Authority of a small city in upstate New York. A group of tenants had tried to organize but failed. One of the mothers suggested that maybe they needed help.

"But who can we ask to help us? Why would anybody take an interest in our problems? After all, we're just housewives. Nobody's going to take an interest in us."

The woman who suggested the idea thought that a labor union might be helpful. A friend was a member of the union in a nearby paper-box plant. She would ask him.

The friend agreed to speak to his shop steward. The shop steward spoke to the president of the local. The president of the local knew a teacher at the labor relations school of a nearby university. The name of a woman professor was passed down from president to shop steward to union member to friend. At the next meeting of the tenants, it was decided that a letter ought to be written, asking for help.

"We need your help to tell us what to do. The janitor doesn't keep up the buildings. When our relief checks come, the landlord gets them first. Children are running wild. We are afraid somebody's going to get hurt. We don't know who to talk to. Maybe you can tell us."

The lady professor promptly replied to the letter and offered to attend the next tenants' meeting. When she did, she spent the first hour of the meeting listening to the members' individual complaints. The committee president was an elderly lady. She did not try to exercise control over the meeting. In fact, the only action the committee had ever taken was to write a letter to the superintendent of the project. It had not been answered. Finally, the lady professor spoke up.

"My friends, I have listened to your story and I understand the problems that you have been having in this housing project. But as far as I can make out, you haven't done anything to change the situation. Why don't we make a list of the things you would like to change? And then we will decide what we can do. After all, unless you try, you will never know."

With her guidance, the group agreed that their primary complaints had to do with the janitor service in their building, that the superintendent got their welfare checks before they did, that nobody seemed interested in talking about how they could control the children in the project. These three things were of primary concern.

"Let's start by writing a letter to the chairman of the Housing Authority," their adviser suggested.

"How can we do that?" they asked. "He would never read our letter. Anyway how do we write such a letter?"

The adviser answered: "We can do that right now. Does anyone have a typewriter?" (No one did.) "Does anyone have a piece of stationery?" (Negative.) "Well, how about a piece of paper?" (Paper and pen were found.) "Let's begin. If you can decide what your letter is going to say, I will have it typed up in my office and send it to you for you all to sign. Then you will have to mail it. You ought to receive a reply promptly. Is everyone here willing to sign?" After further discussion, they all agreed to put their names on the letter, except for two women who felt that their handwriting was so bad that they did not want to sign. Another lady agreed to sign their names for them.

The letter was written, with the help of the adviser. When it was typed up and signed by all the ladies, they mailed it to the chairman of the housing authority.

Two weeks went by. No letter was received from the chairman. When the president of the committee reported this at the next meeting, the lady professor agreed to call the chairman's office.

"What do you mean," the chairman's assistant replied. "We received that letter two weeks ago and answered it on the following day. I have a carbon of our reply in front of me. Your committee must have received it by now."

On a hunch, the adviser asked the president of the committee to look in her mailbox.

"What mailbox," the president asked. "I get all my mail from the superintendent. He brings it to my apartment. That's when he gives me my welfare check—I didn't know I had a mailbox."

The adviser told the president to go to the superintendent and ask for a key to her mailbox. Sure enough, the reply from the Housing Authority was there. The chairman had promised that a representative of the Housing Authority would meet with the tenant's committee at their convenience. He had given the name of the man who should be contacted.

From there on, things moved more quickly. A meeting was held with the deputy director of the department of community relations of the Housing Authority. The superintendent of the project attended the meeting. One of the more articulate members of the committee presented the grievances of the group. The representative of the housing authority responded to each proposal.

Some of the problems were resolved on the spot. The superintendent was directed to give every tenant a key to the mailbox and not to interfere with the mail system. A letter was written to the local post office, directing the postman to place the mail in the mailboxes without notifying the superintendent. The Authority also agreed to inspect the project to determine whether the janitor service was adequate.

After a series of inspections, it was decided that the janitor was not doing his job. He was transferred to another project where he would be supervised.

The problem of the children proved to be difficult. The Authority agreed to provide a part-time youth worker to work with a teen-age gang operating in the project, and to provide recreation activities for the younger children.

Another setting for emerging group conflict involves parents who seek more power over their local public schools. In New York City, the Board of Education established several local school committees elected from within the community. A dispute arose as to whether that committee should have the power to dismiss teachers who were unacceptable to it. Before the dispute was resolved, the teachers had gone out on strike, the schools were closed, the community was in an uproar, and the principle of local autonomy was in doubt.

The efforts of parent organizations, in seeking to bargain effectively with school administrators for improvements in the quality of education, particularly in urban centers, present a case history in frustration. In a small community, the P.T.A. or informal pressure groups of parents can bring about significant changes because of the close personal relationships between individual parents and the school administrator. Within large cities, the system becomes impersonal. Local control becomes increasingly difficult as the system expands.

The experiment in New York was made possible through a foundation grant, and after great pressure upon community leaders through militant direct-action techniques on the part of local parent groups. The tremendous effort required to bring about experimentation in a few of the New York public school districts should warn other parent groups of the problems that will confront them in other metropolitan public school systems.

Nevertheless, it is quite clear that the community cannot exert effective power upon the school system until it has achieved a representative status. Where attempts are made to institutionalize decentralization to deliberately strengthen the voice of local parents, new confrontations will erupt in which impersonal administrative efficiency collides with demands from the parents for autonomy and increased power. Unless the parents have a right to bring the school board to the bargaining table, they have little chance of realizing significant gains.

How to Control an Existing Organization

Sometimes you will discover that an organization already exists that could help you resolve your dispute, or achieve an objective. Often, an existing organization has been established for exactly the purpose you contemplate, and is available for use. How can your leverage be combined with that of others?

Individuals and organizations may be involved in other projects which do not interest you. The challenge may be to take hold of the existing pattern of interest and mold it into an effective instrument through which to achieve your own design.

For the record, there are over three thousand national

trade associations in the United States, most of them concerned
with particular industries. Many are well known, like the
United States Chamber of Commerce, The American Bankers
Association, The American Bar Association, and the American
Medical Association. Others are less well known: at random,
The Scientific Apparatus Makers Association, The National As-
sociation of Electronic Organ Manufacturers, and The Inter-
national Bridge, Tunnel & Turnpike Association.

An understanding of the potential use of these groups and
others can be useful if you are shopping for power levers.

For example, a storekeeper in a deteriorating neighborhood was mugged outside his store by three knife-wielding
heroin addicts. He decided to try to improve the police protection in the neighborhood. He went about it in a methodical
way. He looked up the names of the commercial organizations,
merchants' associations, and other community groups in his
neighborhood. He called each group on the telephone and
invited them to send a representative to his house for a meeting.
About a dozen persons attended. First, he described what had
happened to him. Then, he reported on local crime statistics.
He cited a police report which showed that robberies and
crimes of violence had been increasing.

"What are we going to do about it?" he asked the business
group. "If we act together, we represent a substantial part of the
business community. I would suggest that each organization
write letters to the mayor, police commissioner, and city council members and assemblymen representing this district, asking
them to provide increased police protection. Then a delegation
should meet with the mayor and the police commissioner to
see whether we can't get a commitment for more policemen."

They thought his suggestion was excellent, and followed
the plan exactly as he had detailed it. Within a month, the
newspapers announced that the number of patrolmen in the
precinct was being doubled, with five new prowl cars assigned.

Where organizations are already likely to be enthusiastic
about a particular project, you can often goad them into
precipitate action. But sometimes you may have to make
changes. You may have to gain control.

Where leadership of an organization is not responsive to
the underlying wishes of the membership, it may even be possible for a few members to carry out a successful raid. This

can be done by surprise. If incumbents have not protected themselves, it may be possible to "pack" the annual meeting with members who desire a change in leadership.

An example of this recently occurred in a trade association. Members from one segment of the industry had been systematically excluded from chairmanships. At the annual meeting, an unusually large number of members appeared. After the official slate of officers was nominated, one of the insurgents nominated a contesting slate. Although the chairman tried to postpone the vote, the insurgents, by a healthy majority of the members present, elected their slate.

A member may run as an insurgent candidate by finding an issue that will provide enough support to get him elected. An example was William F. Buckley's campaign for the Board of Trustees of Yale University. He held that the university should give preference to the children of alumni in its admissions policy. Since the voting constituency is made up of alumni, many of whom have sons who would like to go to Yale, it would have been natural to expect widespread sympathy for Mr. Buckley. Unfortunately, he lost to a stronger candidate. A similar tactic can be used in other situations. The organization member who wants a seat on the board for private purposes should carefully evaluate the make-up of the membership. Is there any common purpose that will guarantee support to a candidate? What is needed to win?

In a recent election in a trade association, the officers had spent association funds on a lavish meeting in the Bahamas. One of their opponents sent Xerox copies of the hotel bill to the membership, with a typical dinner menu and three pictures of the incumbent candidates whooping it up with bar girls. The response at the polls was overwhelming. Now the officers pay their own expenses and meet in a nearby motel.

Another common issue is the alleged failure of the incumbents to carry out the objectives of the organization. Tension often exists between the "ins" and "outs." If this potential is fanned into a blaze, a raid may be possible. The voluntary organization that fails to respond to the changing needs of potential members, or that fails to create new constituencies by embracing programs for which there is a potential demand, may wither away for lack of achievement and be replaced by more responsive leaders.

Many voluntary organizations whose leadership has become complacent and has failed to keep in step with the times have suddenly found that an opposition slate was being organized to make a fight at the annual election. And whether or not the insurgents succeed in taking over the organization, even the threat of such membership revolt will bring about dramatic changes in the behavior of those elected to office.

Failing election, if you want to capture an organization and ride away with it, you should analyze the differences between the "formal" and the "real" structure in order to ascertain whose hands hold the reins and how they can be snatched away. Sometimes, the formal structure will turn out to be irrelevant—the organization will be dominated by a few powerful persons who stand "off stage." Then for all practical purposes, you can disregard the formalities and concentrate your efforts upon these key people, trying to persuade them to issue necessary instructions.

If you are contemplating a takeover, a word of caution. The best laid plans can sometimes be thwarted. One organization had fallen under the influence of its "young turks." At the next meeting, they proposed several radical changes. It seemed almost inevitable that their program would be approved. But one long-time director, by elaborating on the dangers of expansion, possible increased costs, risks of unknown liabilities, and other latent difficulties, deflated the enthusiasm of the uncommitted members. He persuaded them to abandon the entire program.

"After all," he concluded, "even if the proposals now being made by our new officers may in the long run turn out to be exactly what is best for our organization, surely we have the right to ask them to proceed cautiously, to study the questions we have raised to be sure that they fully understand the inherent dangers that we have pointed out, and to establish to the satisfaction of all the members that these important changes are really in our best interest. I am not asking the membership to vote against these proposals. I am only asking that our leaders exercise caution, that they do no come to us with sweeping suggestions that have not had the benefit of exacting review by those of us who feel a personal responsibility for guiding the future of this organization. Therefore, I ask the membership to vote that these proposals be tabled until the next meeting."

This case was unusual. When a faction of a membership has the votes and controls the committee chairmanships, it is usually quite able to put through its program.

It is not necessary to take over the organization in every aspect. It is working control that is important, the ability to influence the organization's activities in those areas that are important to you, without regard to any responsibility or direction over other activities that may be irrelevant to your purposes.

It is possible for a small group of members to infiltrate an organization. Members who conscientiously serve on committees are soon appointed to official positions within the hierarchy. Within a few years, hard-working members will be raised to positions of responsibility. Voluntary organizations are particularly susceptible to such infiltration because dedicated members are hard to find. Active members move ahead rapidly. When the insurgent group has gained access to a body that determines significant policy, it is possible to change the organization's program.

You should not forget the paid staff in organization affairs. The staff can be particularly important to any member who wants to use the organization for some purpose of his own. The inchoate desire of a paid staff to see its organization prosper will usually guarantee a welcome to any member who promises growth. "I don't give a damn what you want to do," one staff member said. "As long as you do something to stir up this organization, I will support you. We need new ideas and new programs. The more we do, the better I like it."

Often, in return for help in reaching other organizational goals, the staff will trade away to a hard-working member an opportunity to participate in policy decisions. For example, a member who works hard on a membership drive, or on making a success of the annual meeting, will be given a seat on a policy-making committee or will have an opportunity to make his voice known to the top officers of the organization. This transaction is often carried out through the executive director of the organization.

Once you have working control of an organization, you can direct it against your opponent. In this effort, you should be sure that the impact of the organization is maximized by using its potential as efficiently as possible.

The Intelligent Use of Direct Action Tactics

As soon as the organization has decided to engage in a conflict situation, it should begin to make its plans for the campaign. You will want to be a part of the planning group.

The problems of tooling up an organization for a conflict situation are often the same no matter what kind of group is involved or what kind of dispute engages its attention. The group has to make precise plans, appraise its options, marshal its resources, and decide exactly who will carry out the campaign and how they will proceed.

Each side will have different weapons available. Bargaining advantages are gained by aggressive use of public relations and by relentless, assertive demands by the petitioner. On the other hand, a strong defensive posture through the power of delay, and by reliance upon management prerogatives are tools of the institution. An additional need of groups that wish to involve themselves in conflict situations is competent legal advice, in advance. Almost any form of direct action involves a willingness to take risks. But no individual and no organization should takes risks blindly, as did one organization that attempted to hold a fund-raising rally in a public park in Florida. It discovered too late that it was violating a municipal ordinance—the meeting concluded at the city jail, and all the officers were heavily fined. The net loss of the affair amounted to $12,000.

A citizens' committee to fight water pollution squared off against an industrial plant that was dumping raw waste into a lake. What were the options? It could petition the officers and directors of the corporation. It could place an advertisement in the newspapers or buy time on radio and television in order to direct the attention of the public to the source of pollution. It could stage an "incident" at the site of the dumping. Women and children picketing the overflow would likely be given space in the newspapers and appear on local television. On the other hand, the committee could bring pressure to bear through political representatives. The government agency responsible for regulating water pollution might be another likely target. The citizens' committee could institute a lawsuit or petition to the appropriate administrative agency. The stockholders of the corporation might also be involved in the campaign. A boycott of the company's products might be feasible. If all these tactics were executed simultaneously, their cumulative effort might be greater than any single step.

In the meantime, what is going through the mind of the corporation president? Does he think that this irritating campaign will continue indefinitely? Probably not. Perhaps the business interests involved will count on riding out a temporary public indignation.

The committee may have to adopt a tactic that will destroy the company's inclination to postpone action. A threat to obtain a court order against the pollution unless the situation is remedied by a certain date would be one such tactic. Or a negotiating committee might go to the corporation president with a threat of using the comprehensive plan enumerated above for publicizing the situation, unless a suitable arrangement could be reached by a certain date. These tactics would be intended to create a deadline and the contingent penalties will have to be severe enough to persuade the president that additional plant investment is more attractive than facing whatever the committee threatens.

How effective these methods will be depends upon the situation, the organization's strength, and the public support of its goals. When goals are unpopular, however, remember that power can be supplemented by money and manpower.

In the area of civil rights, the movement has been chronically short of funds. Civil rights leaders have not been successful in harnessing the potential power of block voting. Underfinanced and lacking broad political power, they had to turn to other methods. Sometimes these tactics worked, sometimes not. Lacking more conventional power outlets, minority groups were forced to innovate.

In *Legal Restraints on Racial Discrimination in Employment*, Michael Sovern tells how the threat of direct action was needed to initiate the "long slow march." In the early 1940's Negroes wondered when the depression would end for them. They fixed their hopes on the President. But the President did not act until almost a million Negroes threatened to march on Washington to protest against the exclusion of Negroes from employment in government and defense industries. Only then, on June 25, 1941, did the President sign Executive Order 8802,

prohibiting discrimination in government and defense industries.

So it was in the beginning. And direct action has been necessary many times since. How effective has it been? Tools bor-
rowed from the labor movement—sit-ins, boycotts, and violence
—have been used by civil rights activists. Sovern suggests that,
even now, in spite of the apparent willingness by industry to
accept change, mere petition does not achieve significant gains.
Direct action is necessary. But the action had better be intelligent and well advised. It was lacking in the following example.

In April, 1966, a militant civil rights group in San Francisco
began to picket the Sheraton Palace Hotel to obtain a fair employment agreement. A negotiating meeting was held with local
NAACP and CORE chapters on May 16, 1966. Present, among
others, were representatives of the San Francisco Human Rights
Commission and officers of the Hotel Association. Union representatives were invited, but did not attend.

As to union participation, the CORE representative remarked: "I don't give a damn about labor unions."

At subsequent meetings, a draft proposal was considered.
The Hotel Association sent a copy to the union. Finally, in
July, a rumor was received that a mob would march on the
hotel. The chief of police warned that he did not have enough
manpower to protect the hotels and that it would be a mistake
for him to try to obtain more manpower because, in his opinion,
San Francisco was "about to go up in flames." Neither the
mayor nor Governor Brown could be reached.

On July 22, the Hotel Association caved in and signed a
draft agreement to improve job ratios in the hiring of minority
groups, to notify the Urban League, PACT, and other employment sources of available jobs, to actively recruit workers from
minority groups, and to provide information periodically on the
ratios of minority group workers in the work force. In return,
the demonstrations were canceled.

But the victory was illusory. On its face, it appeared to be
a successful exercise in power bargaining. Such was not the case:
The San Francisco Joint Executive Board of the hotel workers'
unions filed a grievance under its collective bargaining contract.
This issue went to arbitration before Robert Burns, a labor
arbitrator, who held that the Hotel Association had violated its

union contract by entering into a conflicting contract with the civil rights group. He found that the 1966 agreement was obtained under duress, that it interfered with the vested rights of the employees of the hotels under their union contracts. "The purpose of the agreement was to establish a preference for Negroes," Burns held. That purpose was unlawful, and the agreement was void. The civil rights groups were back where they started. Under the National Labor Relations Act, only the union can be the "exclusive representative."

This case suggests that organizations that use direct action to achieve group objectives should carefully study the rules of the game in advance. It would appear from hindsight that the Negro leaders, by ignoring the union's stake in the dispute, sacrificed the advantage they had won. Had the union been a party to the arrangement, the improvements in job entry for Negroes might have been permanent.

No matter how much raw power a civil rights group is able to exert through direct action, real gains will not be achieved unless valid contractual commitments have been obtained. Negotiators had better be sure that their opponents will have to stand behind any commitment made by its representatives.

A situation that occurred in Rochester, New York, is exemplary. A militant civil rights group called FIGHT had been trying to get the Eastman Kodak Company to increase the job openings for hard-core minority unemployed. This contest, which was well documented in the press, used militant, direct action negotiating techniques. The FIGHT organization was led by an emotional and articulate minister, Franklin Florence, and advised by Saul Alinsky, a prominent professional agitator.

The first confrontation between Florence and the Kodak Company took place on September 2, 1966. At the initial meeting, Florence pointed out that his group spoke for "unemployable" minority members. The company appeared to be sympathetic and explained its policy regarding open employment. A second meeting was scheduled two weeks later. FIGHT submitted a written demand that Kodak hire six hundred unemployables. Kodak refused to be bound by such a figure, but did agree to expand its training programs for unskilled workers, and solicited job candidates. The talks dragged on for two more meetings. FIGHT charged that Kodak was stalling, and began to escalate press conferences and propaganda in an attempt to obtain a firm commitment from Kodak on exactly how many workers would be accepted.

During the fall of 1966, the conflict deepened. In December, an assistant vice president, seeking to achieve a better relationship with FIGHT, got permission from his boss to initiate a new series of discussions. Two days of negotiations took place and at the end of the second day an agreement was reached. Kodak, represented by the assistant vice president, agreed to hire six hundred unemployable minority workers within a twenty-four-month period. The agreement was announced by FIGHT as a great victory.

But within an hour the president of Kodak, learning of the terms of the agreement, repudiated it. On the following day, the executive committee of the company declared the agreement unauthorized. FIGHT charged that a promise had been broken. And the new dispute escalated the differences between the parties to new heights. At the annual meeting of the Kodak Company the controversy captured national attention. Reverend Florence and his supporters picketed the meeting and issued press releases accusing the company of bad faith. Alinsky claimed that his forces had obtained an advantage from the company's revocation of the agreement. FIGHT then asked for one thousand two hundred jobs rather than the original six hundred.

In disputes which involve the inflammatory demands of whole communities all the traditional skills for dealing with less bitter but no less important controversies should be made available to help resolve the destructive confrontations between ever more violent disputants.

There have been many instances where rational dispute settlement has been used to ease the way for inevitable social change. A young engineer was appointed plant manager of a furniture factory in the South. He discovered that his predecessors had gone to elaborate lengths to assure that no Negro employees would work on the same production line as white employees. Certain parts of the operation were functioning inefficiently for this reason. When the new manager pointed out that this practice was contrary to good engineering procedures, he was told that no other system would be acceptable. "The men won't go along with any change," he was told.

He reported the situation to his home office and was given authority to make changes. He suspected that he would not be able to make a change without coming into conflict with those who preferred the present system. He was right. At his first staff meeting, at which the impending reorganization was discussed, he was able to identify the supervisor who was most committed to *de facto* segregation. How could he persuade this man that change was necessary? He addressed his staff:

"I have been asked to streamline the operation of our production line. Toward that end, I am going to form a task force to study the problem and recommend a solution. Mr. Jones [the segregationist] will be chairman of that task force, and I will want a report by next Friday on how we can have the most efficient operation from an engineering point of view. The task force will have to be able to justify any changes that are made, both economically and from the point of view of simplifying the operation. Is that understood?"

The newly appointed chairman of the task force went to work. He was a competent production man and soon recognized that the only way the plant could be organized efficiently was to eliminate the unofficial barrier between races. He designed an efficient production line, giving up any attempt to continue the segregated pattern of work assignments. On the following Friday, the plant manager complimented the chairman on the skill with which he had carried out his assignment and directed the staff to put the change into effect.

And in another setting, mediation made it possible to avoid a destructive impasse between impatient students and an immovable university president. Militant student activists had called a strike against their college, basing their grievance on a number of seemingly minor complaints against the administration. The president promptly dismissed the ringleaders, advising their parents that the college could not tolerate their behavior.

Now the students had a real issue: Was the discipline justified? The number of students who stayed away from classes suddenly increased, and the strikers were joined by some of the younger members of the faculty. Various acts of vandalism ensued. The alumni of the college began to take sides on the issues.

Just at the point when the dispute appeared ready to explode into violence, harsh retaliatory police action, and a dose of bad national publicity, a local labor mediator offered his services. However, it was arranged for a faculty committee to invite the mediator into the controversy. His appointment was publicized. The mediator then met with various student leaders, and privately with the president. He discovered that the students' primary aim was to present their grievances personally to the president. The mediator persuaded the president to participate in a joint mediation session. This was arranged in the board room of the college trustees. One by one, the student activists came forward and unburdened themselves. A wide range of grievances was presented, some conflicting, some patently absurd. After the students made their presentations, the president responded, discussing each suggestion in turn.

The mediator had previously ascertained that if one or two minor concessions were made regarding the service in the college cafeteria and scheduling of extracurricular events, most of the students would be satisfied. He also believed that a better method of communication between students and administration could be developed to avoid similar problems in the future, and had prevailed on the president to agree to establish a joint faculty-student council that would serve as a sounding board for student complaints. The president announced the formation of such a group and called for a student election to determine which student leaders would represent their interests on the board. He announced the names of the faculty members in accordance with a list that he and the mediator had prepared following their consultation with the faculty.

What could have degenerated into a bloody and unpleasant impasse was resolved without a blow.

CONCLUSION

"I plan to retire," the tired-looking businessman said. "When I started my business, everything was simple. The income tax was just beginning. No withholding. No unemployment insurance. No union. The government didn't bother me. I had a good product and good customers. Not anymore. Now everything has changed. I have problems that didn't exist thirty years ago. There are just too many fights. I've had enough."

The world is changing. People are multiplying at a savage rate. Disagreements are increasing even faster. We are being drowned in a sea of unpleasant and irreconcilable controversies. What to do?

I have urged disputants to resolve disagreements between themselves, as quickly as possible. They should do this for selfish reasons, to reduce the cost of resolution. But they would also eliminate unnecessary work for the nation's courts. Rather than impoverish the quality of justice dispensed by courts, it seems preferable to encourage businessmen and other litigants to avoid them. The various techniques that have been described are among the most promising vehicles for the relief of would-be litigants.

There are those who have always resolved their controversies privately, and continue to urge their lawyers to avoid the courts.

One of my close friends at law school, now the president of a national corporation, is one. He once told me: "I never intend to practice law. My aim is to learn how a business enter-

215

prise can protect its profitability. I don't want to win law
cases against other businessmen, or against the government. I
want to avoid them. I went to law school to learn how to avoid
conflict."

He is a great believer in out-of-court solutions. He believes
that the technological explosion is liberating the businessman
by making more opportunities available. He wants to take advantage of them. He does not want to waste his time squabbling
over contractual disagreements.

This sensible point of view is equally valid for the individual. Almost any human activity is more profitable than
worrying a dreary lawsuit through the courts. More often than
not, some better method for resolution can be found than
forcing an opponent to try his case in court. Most of the available alternatives involve one form or another of negotiated
settlement or some privately agreed-upon resolution technique.
All of the examples I have described in this book should be
thought of as providing dispute settlement skills through which
the reader can force a satisfactory solution without the need
for going to court.

I do not suggest that every dispute should be compromised,
or that anyone should give away his legitimate rights. Private
settlement techniques can be used aggressively and can often
result in a better deal for the bargainer than he could possibly
receive in court. There is nothing weak about the hard-nosed
union negotiator who forces an employer to sign a collective
bargaining contract under the threat of a mutually disastrous
strike. The corporate executive who uses the full heft of his
company's economic power to force a supplier to give him a
quantity discount is certainly not an impractical idealist. In
the same way, the individual who uses effective techniques for
bringing pressure to bear upon an opponent, and obtains a
satisfactory settlement of an impending dispute, can only be
looked upon with approval in the sense that anyone who can
achieve his ends without burdening the courts ought to be com-
mended.

But perhaps congratulations are not necessary. Such success
carries its own reward. Parties are more content with the results of a voluntary settlement and more committed to it than
parties who have won or lost because of the intervention of an
outside authority. The loser of a lawsuit is generally a bitter

man. But parties who have completed a successful negotiation are customarily photographed in an atmosphere of handshakes, cigars, and smiles. The contrast is meaningful.

In one attempt to resolve a substantial corporate lawsuit, the attorneys were called before a federal judge. In his chambers, they spent two full days trying to design a formula that would be acceptable to their respective corporate clients.

Finally it appeared that no compromise would be reached, although both sides were willing to make substantial concessions. The stumbling block concerned which corporation would be obligated to pay a finder's fee of less than $20,000. Neither corporation was willing either to admit that it had retained the finder or share the responsibility for compensating him.

The judge then ordered the lawyers to bring their clients before him, and urged the chief executives of both companies to resolve the final issue.

One company president, a plain-spoken man who had worked on the factory floor of the corporation's original plant, listened intently. When the judge was through, this man spoke up: "Gentlemen, either we come to an agreement today and walk out of this room as successful negotiators or, by God, we're going to talk ourselves into more anguish, more expense, more explaining, and more ill will than any one of us could produce intentionally in a year of hard work. I suggest to you that $10,000 is a small price to pay for coming out of this room a hero. Aren't you fellows willing to swap a small principle for a deal? Let's write off this finder's fee for the piece of dirty garbage that it is, split it right down the middle, and tell the judge we've settled. How about it?"

Put in those terms, the president of the other corporation had to agree that the logic of settlement was inescapable. With the federal judge smiling his approval, the relieved businessmen and their lawyers warmly shook hands, congratulated each other upon their statesmanship, and happily sauntered back to their offices.

Consider the alternative. If this settlement had not been reached, threats would have been exchanged across the table. Further time would have been wasted, both in thrashing out the issue of the finder's fee and reawakening several other issues. The case might finally have been tried. Almost inevitably, an appeal would have been taken from the trial court's decision.

Each of the lawyers and responsible executives would have had to answer increasingly impatient questions from their superiors. The presidents of the companies would have been subjected to questions by their boards of directors, and further questions at stockholders' meetings: "Why can't this unpleasant litigation be settled?" "Who's to blame?"

By agreeing to split the difference on the finder's fee, the parties avoided all the potential turmoil, disruption, and displeasure. The sun shines upon those individuals and businessmen who are able to achieve solutions to unpleasant and seemingly irreconcilable controversies. All that is needed is intelligence and the willingness to use those weapons which are most likely to bring results.

INDEX